Collins

SMART TECH

2

Manasi Kashikar
Sneha Krishnan

Student + Teacher				Teacher-only	
a animations	**ia** activities	**g** games		**lp** lesson plans	**tn** teacher's notes
ilt instructor-led tutorials	**w** worksheets	**v** videos		**w** worksheets	**ak** answer keys
	audio				

PREFACE

Over the last few decades, technology has surrounded almost all aspects of our lives. It is remarkable that the pace at which technology evolves has also accelerated. In India, smartphones and the internet have become widely accessible, putting the power of technology in the hands of millions.

In this backdrop, we believe that it is important for students to:

- understand that technology is going to keep evolving, and it is a life skill to learn.
- know the basics of coding, which makes devices come to life. Coding skills are as essential today as basic Math and Language skills.
- take control of regulating their usage and make constructive use of their access to computer devices.

The ***Collins Smart Tech*** series adheres to the vision of the National Education Policy 2020. Through the series, we endeavour to acquaint students with technology in a way that is relatable, engaging and fun. Using Windows 10 and MS Office 2016, students are introduced to widely used tools. The series introduces computational thinking from class 2 onwards with the intent of developing the necessary skills that students need to acquire coding skills. The chapters on coding skills help students understand the logic behind the code and develop their own problem-solving and critical thinking abilities. The focus is on developing critical thinking and inquiry and enabling discovery-, discussion- and analysis-based teaching and learning methods for holistic education.

Now, children have exposure to computer devices and the internet from a young age. Basis our experience at MindChamp, students need to understand concepts in their context and not in an isolated fashion. Therefore, we have attempted to provide real-life instances that they can easily relate with as much as possible. Even topics such as AI, VR, AR and IoT have been covered with, the same zeal. This stands true for the theoretical as well as the practical aspects of the chapters. It is our sincere hope that teachers find imparting knowledge from this series as exciting as students learning from it.

Finally, we aspire to set a precedent for high-quality Computer Science education across the country that keeps up with the changes in technology. Observations, experiences, suggestions and critique from teachers and students alike act as our guide in carrying forward this aspiration.

We would like to thank our interns Janita George, Nisha Gokhale and Srinath K Nallamalli in helping us shape the content.

Key Features

What will I learn?

Outlines well-defined learning objectives in the form of questions that describe what students will learn in the chapter

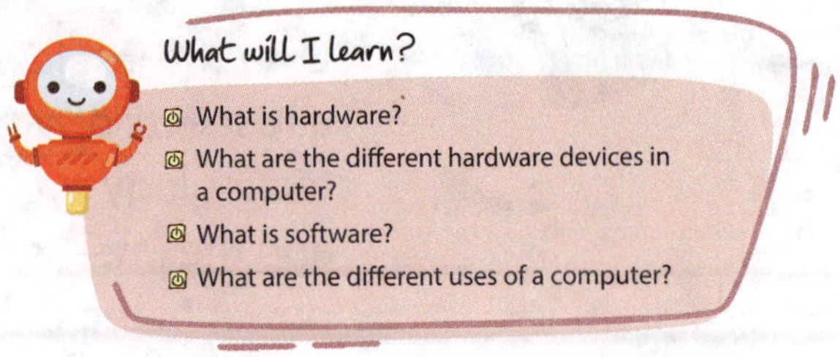

Think and Discuss

Includes various activities and real-life examples to set the context for what students are about to learn

Knowledge Bytes

Contains additional information/facts about the topic being taught

Meaning

Gives contextual meaning of difficult words

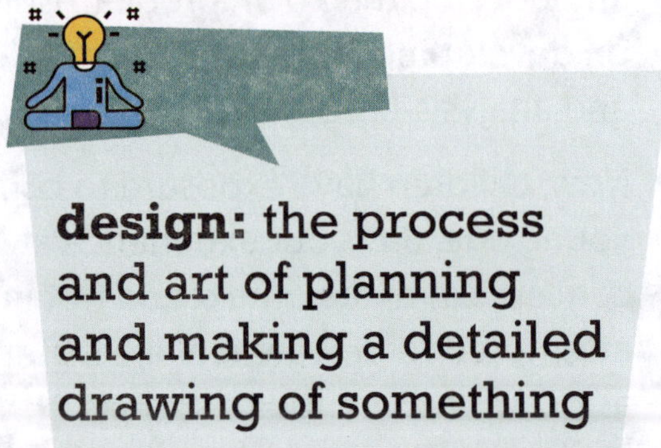

I am smart!

Provides tips and shortcut tricks for the topics covered in the chapter to foster inquiry- and discovery-based learning

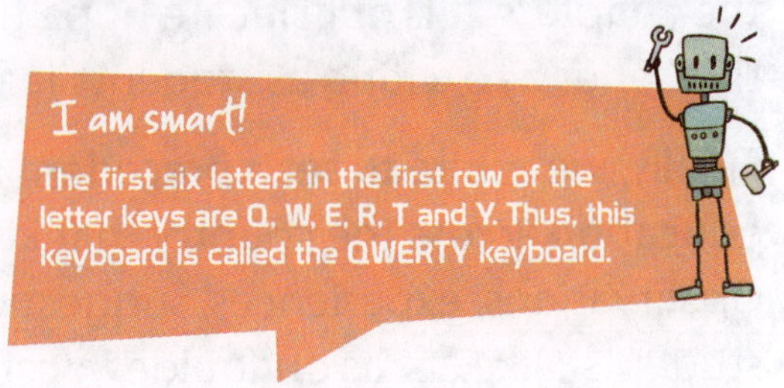

I can do!

Includes hands-on tasks for revision, based on the desired learning outcomes

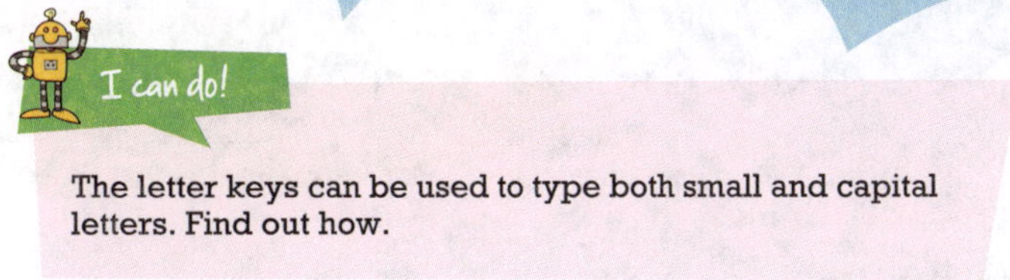

I can do!

The letter keys can be used to type both small and capital letters. Find out how.

I can tell!

Comprises short questions to reinforce the concept learnt and promote competency based education

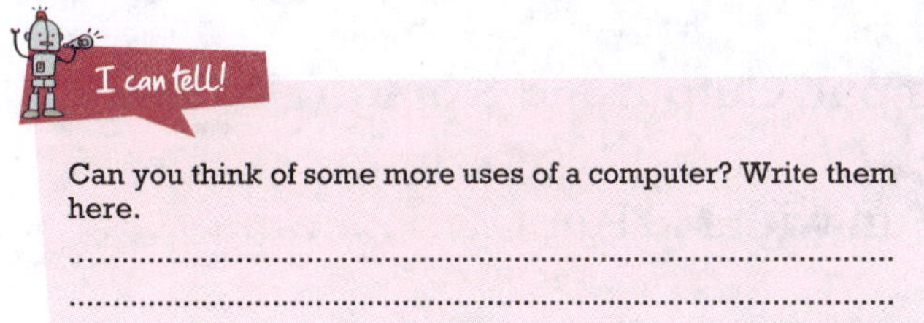

I can tell!

Can you think of some more uses of a computer? Write them here.

....

....

What did I learn?

Revisits all the important points learnt in the chapter

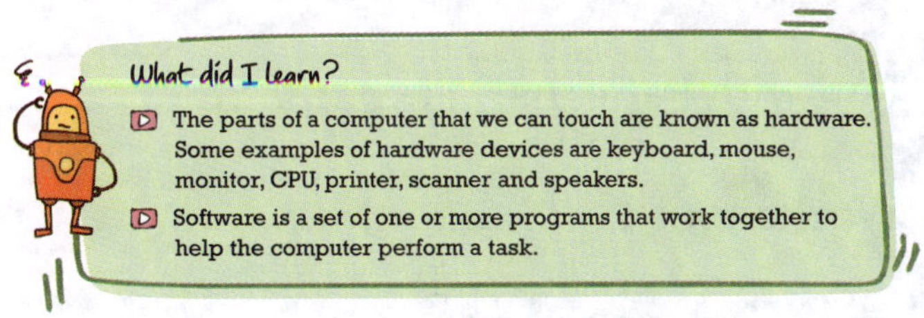

What did I learn?

- The parts of a computer that we can touch are known as hardware. Some examples of hardware devices are keyboard, mouse, monitor, CPU, printer, scanner and speakers.
- Software is a set of one or more programs that work together to help the computer perform a task.

Exercises

Includes exhaustive revision exercises comprising a blend of both objective-type and detailed-answer type questions. Questions based on programming teach how to use and integrate technology in everyday life.

Exercises

1. State whether the following statements are true (T) or false (F).

   a. Mouse has a long wire connected to the CPU box.

Lab Activity

Tests the practical application of the concepts taught to enhance comprehension and provide opportunities for peer tutoring

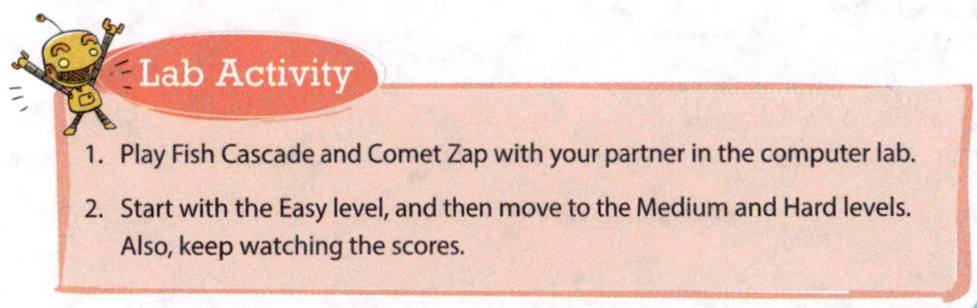

Lab Activity

1. Play Fish Cascade and Comet Zap with your partner in the computer lab.
2. Start with the Easy level, and then move to the Medium and Hard levels. Also, keep watching the scores.

Worksheets

Comprises additional practice questions and projects to cater to traditional examination requirements

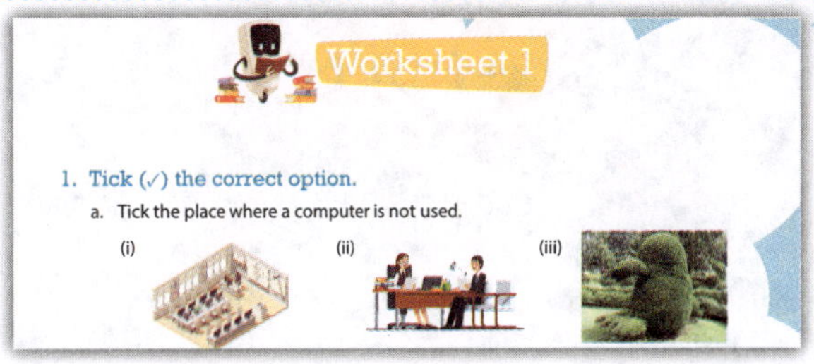

Worksheet 1

1. Tick (✓) the correct option.

   a. Tick the place where a computer is not used.

   (i) (ii) (iii)

Skills section

Focused on a specific skill at each level, this section helps children acquire a skill that will be of use to them in the real world. Also includes hands-on projects to reinforce learning and facilitate cooperation

USING A COMPUTER PROPERLY

1. Sit comfortably with back straight. Do not lean forward or slouch.

Contents

1

Parts and Uses of a Computer

What will I learn?

- What is hardware?
- What are the different hardware devices in a computer?
- What is software?
- What are the different uses of a computer?

Think and Discuss

Tick (✓) the things you can touch.

Plants	Air	Bed
a. 	b. 	c. 
☐	☐	☐
Rainbow	**Printer**	**Tux Paint**
d. 	e. 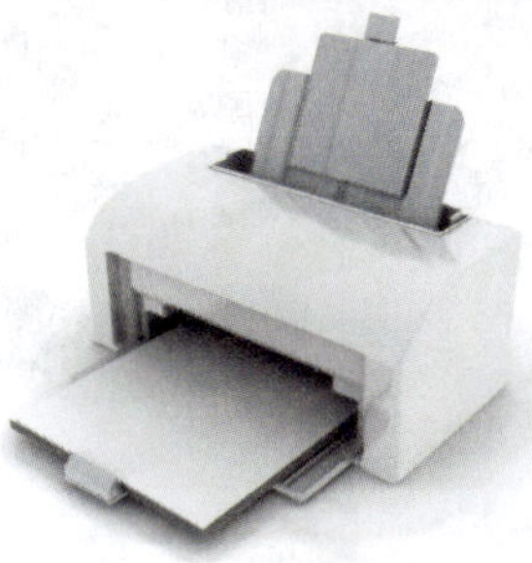	f. 
☐	☐	☐

A computer is a smart machine. It has many parts. Do you remember their names?

HARDWARE

The parts of a computer that we can touch are known as hardware. Keyboard, mouse, monitor, CPU and printer are some examples of hardware devices. We have already learnt about them in Class 1.

The parts of a computer that we can physically touch are known as computer hardware.

I can tell!

Can you name the hardware parts of a computer and label them?

a. ____________________

b. ____________________

c. ____________________

d. ____________________

Let us discuss these in detail.

Monitor

A monitor looks like a TV because it has a screen. It displays the work done on the computer. We can read text, see movies and pictures on the screen. Monitors come in many different shapes and sizes.

Fig. 1.1 *Types of monitors*

There are two types of monitors:

1. Cathode Ray Tube (CRT) monitors
2. Thin Film Transistor (TFT) monitors

I am smart!

A touchscreen helps us to give instructions to the computer by touching it. Mostly, tablets, mobile phones and ATMs have touchscreens. A stylus is a pen-like thing that can be used with a touchscreen instead of fingers.

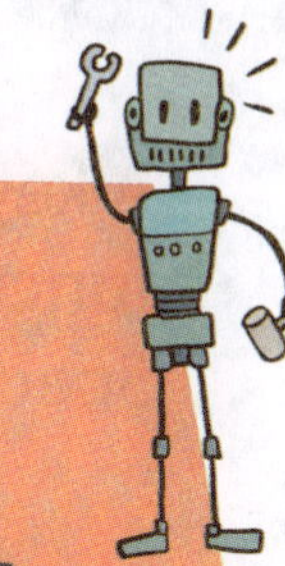

CPU

CPU is the Central Processing Unit. All the processing of data happens in it . The CPU is also known as the processor. All the parts of the computer are connected to the CPU. It controls the other parts of a computer. It is also called the brain of a computer.

The CPU box also consists of:

1. the parts where the computer data is stored.
2. the button for switching the computer on and off.
3. the place where we can attach external hardware devices.

Fig. 1.2 *CPU*

Keyboard

A keyboard is used to enter information into a computer. Without it, sending any information into the computer is difficult.

To write on a computer, we press the keys on the keyboard. This is called **typing**.

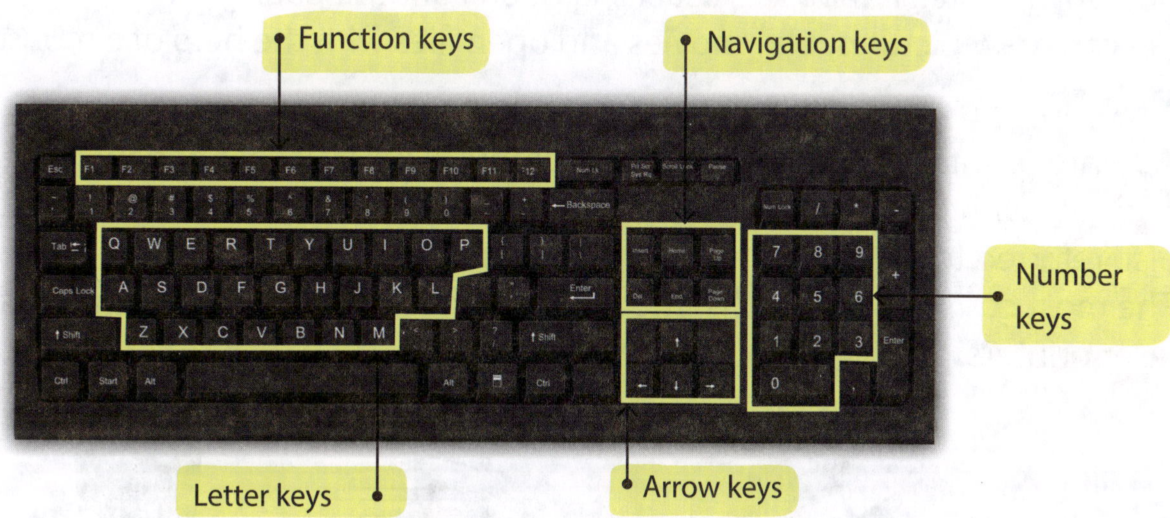

Fig. 1.3 *Keyboard*

A keyboard includes letter keys, number keys, navigation keys, arrow keys, function keys and more keyboard keys like Shift, Caps Lock, Tab, Enter, Spacebar, Esc and Backspace.

Knowledge Bytes

The numeric keypad on the right is made to look like a calculator. The main typing keypad is how a typewriter used to be.

I am smart!

The first six letters in the first row of the letter keys are Q, W, E, R, T and Y. Thus, this keyboard is called the QWERTY keyboard.

I can do!

The letter keys can be used to type both small and capital letters. Find out how.

Hint: Try using Caps Lock and Shift keys along with the letter keys.

Mouse

A mouse is a hardware device that is used to select, point, drag and drop objects on the screen. It has two buttons—*left* or primary button and *right* or secondary button which help us to select objects on the screen. There is a scroll wheel in between the two to move up and down faster. A mouse is usually kept on a mouse pad.

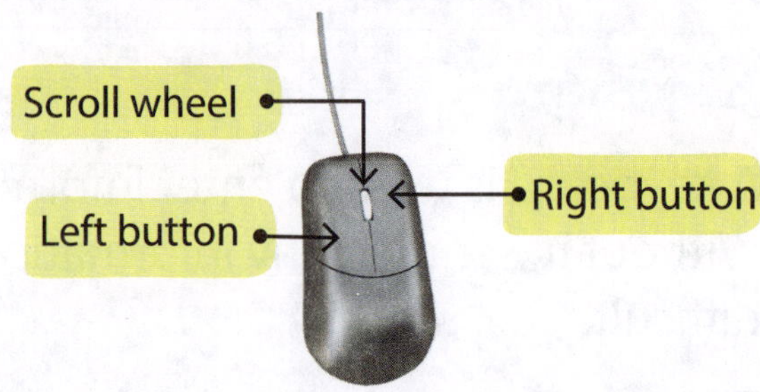

Fig. 1.4 *Mouse*

We can draw pictures, play movies and open files with the help of a mouse.

Printer

A printer prints information from the computer onto a sheet of paper. The sheet of paper with the information printed on it is called the **printout**. Printouts are also referred to as the hard copy of the information.

The most common types of printers are dot matrix printers, inkjet printers and laser printers.

Fig. 1.5 *Types of printers*

Fig 1.6 *Scanner*

Scanner

A scanner can read images or text from a physical item such as a photograph or paper and convert it into a form that the computer understands.

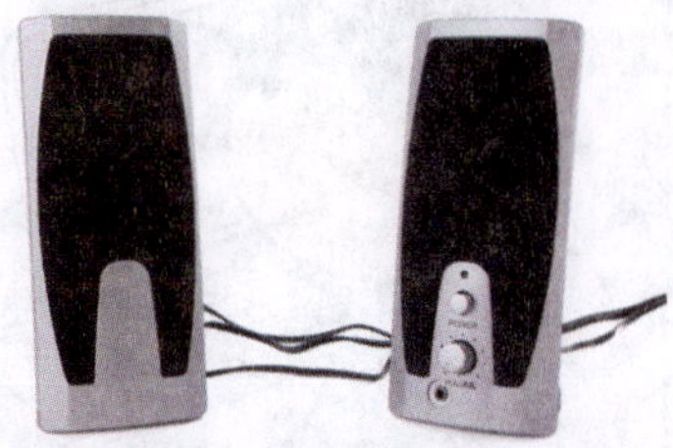

Fig 1.7 *Speakers*

Speakers

Speakers help us listen to the sound played by a computer.

SOFTWARE

In a human body, we can see and touch our hands and legs, but what really keeps us alive is us breathing. Similarly, software keeps the computer alive. A computer is just an empty box without software programs in it. Software is a set of one or more programs that work together to help the computer perform a task. There are two types of software: system software and application software. Let us read more about them.

Software is a set of one or more programs that work together to help the computer perform a task.

System Software

It runs the computer hardware and the system. Windows operating system is an example of system software. It helps to connect the computer hardware with the application software.

Application Software

These are programs that help users do certain tasks. For example, Tux Paint is an application software used to draw and save pictures on a computer.

I can tell!

Discuss with your teacher and classmates about software. Write names of some application and system software.

System software: ....

Application software: ....

USES OF A COMPUTER

A computer is a smart machine that helps us do many things. Different people use computers for different things. Here are some of the ways in which computers are used.

Draw and colour pictures	Do homework/research for projects	Play games

Watch movies	Talk to people far away from us	Listen to music and watch movies

Shop online	Type emails	Solve sums

Places where Computers are Used

	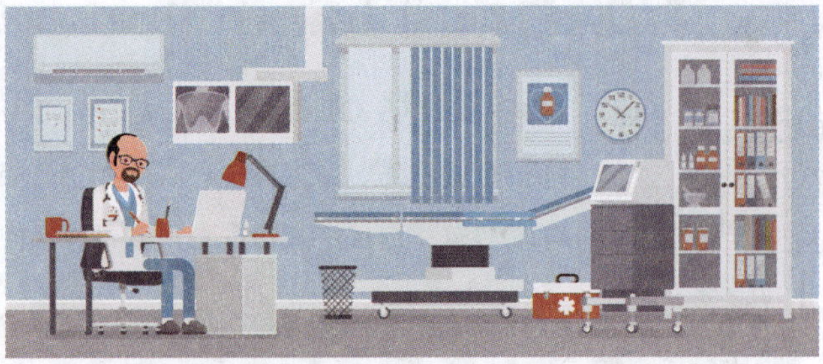
In schools, for teaching and learning.	In hospitals, for doctors to maintain their patients' records.

In banks, to deposit and withdraw money.	In offices, to do official work.

In airports and railway stations, to book tickets and track planes and trains.	In labs, for scientists to do research work.

I can tell!

Can you think of some more uses of a computer? Write them here.

....

....

What did I learn?

- The parts of a computer that we can touch are known as hardware. Some examples of hardware devices are keyboard, mouse, monitor, CPU, printer, scanner and speakers.
- Software is a set of one or more programs that work together to help the computer perform a task.
- System software helps run the computer hardware and the system. Windows operating system is an example of system software.
- Application software are programs that help users do certain tasks. MS Paint is an example of application software.
- Computers are used to draw and colour pictures, play games, watch movies, shop online, type emails, etc.
- Computers are used in schools, hospitals, banks, offices, airports and research labs.

Exercises

1. State whether the following statements are true (T) or false (F).

a. Mouse has a long wire connected to the CPU box. ☐

b. Scanner is a software program. ☐

c. The sheet of paper with information printed on, is called the printout. ☐

d. Monitors help us listen to the sound played by a computer. ☐

e. A computer keyboard is used to type text into the computer. ☐

2. Match the following.

a. Playing games (i) 

b. Watching movies (ii) 

c. Drawing (iii) 

d. Shopping online (iv) 

e. Solving sums (v) 

3. Who am I?

a. I have many keys. ____________________

b. I am a pointing device. ____________________

c. I can give you printouts. ____________________

d. You can watch movies on me. ____________________

e. I can read images or text from a physical item. ____________________

4. Fill in the blanks using the given words.

schools	planes	labs	Offices	Banks

a. ___________ use computers for saving and withdrawing money.

b. In ___________, computers are used for teaching and learning.

c. ___________ use computers for official work.

d. Airports use computers to track ___________.

e. Scientists use computers to do research work in ___________.

5. Put a tick (✓) against the tasks that a computer can do and a cross (×) against the tasks it cannot do.

a. Write letters ☐ b. Wash clothes ☐

c. Feel happy ☐ d. Solve sums ☐

e. Make friends ☐ f. Play music ☐

Lab Activity

1. Find the function of all the keys on the keyboard. Write the names of the keys to:
   a. Move the cursor to the next line in a document ___________
   b. Make all the letters capital ___________
   c. Get the percentage sign (%) ___________
   d. Get question mark (?) ___________
   e. Activate the numeric keypad ___________
2. Try using the mouse by clicking on the right and left buttons.

2

Input, Output and Storage Devices

What will I learn?

- What is the meaning of input and output?
- What are input and output devices?
- What are storage devices?

Think and Discuss

Name these devices. What are they used for?

a.

____

____

____

____

b.

____

____

____

____

c.

____

____

____

____

WHAT IS INPUT AND OUTPUT?

Do you like surprise tests? What if you could ask questions in the test? Imagine your Maths teacher says that you get to ask questions to your friends! When your turn comes, you ask your friend a very simple question: What is the sum of 1 and 2?

Fig. 2.1 *Example of input/output*

You are asking your friend to add two numbers. This means he is taking information. This is known as **input**.

Your friend's brain does the work, that is, to add 1 and 2. This is known as **processing**.

Finally, your friend gives you the answer. This is the result of the question. It is known as **output**.

Similarly, we give input to the computer (1 + 2), the computer processes the input and gives us the output.

> *Input* is information given to a computer.
>
> *Processing* is doing a certain task or action on the input
>
> *Output* is the information that the computer gives to the user after processing.

I can tell!

Which part of the computer does the processing?

Hint: It is also called the brain of computer.

....

Now, let us learn about input and output devices.

INPUT DEVICES

A hardware device that sends input to a computer is called an input device. It is used by the user to give information to the computer.

Input devices give information or input to the computer.

We know that:

- a **keyboard** is used for typing.
- a **mouse** is used for clicking and selecting.
- a **scanner** is used to read images in the computer.

All of these are used to give information to the computer. These are examples of input devices. We will now learn about some more input devices.

Microphone

A microphone is an input device. It is used to record audio into the computer or speak to other users via computers.

Fig. 2.2 *Microphone*

Fig. 2.3 *Joystick*

Joystick

Joystick is an input device. It is used to play video games.

Webcam

A webcam is an input device. It is used to make video calls and take pictures. In desktop computers, it is placed above the monitors for making calls.

Fig. 2.4 *Webcam*

Here are a few input devices. What type of input does each device provide? Write it here.

1. Keyboard ....
2. Scanner ....
3. Webcam ....
4. Microphone ....

OUTPUT DEVICES

The input is processed by the CPU. The computer shows the output to the user.

The hardware device that shows the result to the user is called an output device.

> Output devices show or give the result to the user.

We know that:

- a **monitor** is used to watch movies.
- a **printer** is used to take printouts.
- a **speaker** is used to listen to songs.

All of these are used to give the result to the user. These are examples of output devices. We will now learn about some more output devices.

Headphones

Headphones are a pair of small speakers used for listening to sound without disturbing others. They are safe to use as long as you do not keep them at a high volume.

Fig. 2.5 *Headphones*

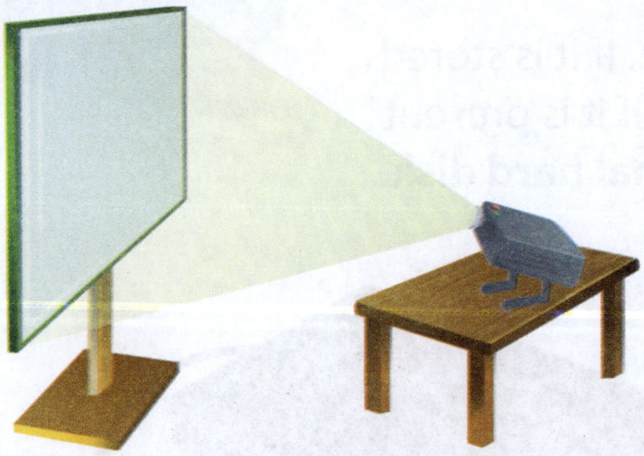

Fig. 2.6 *Projector*

Projector

A projector is a device that projects an image onto a large surface. It is mostly used while giving presentations or playing movies in a theatre.

Plotter

A plotter is a device used for printing big drawings. It uses a pen, pencil or marker to print these drawings.

Fig. 2.7 *Plotter*

I can tell!

Why is a monitor both an input and an output device?

Hint: Think about working of the touchscreens.

....

....

....

Knowledge Bytes

Certain devices which give and take information from the computer are called input-output or I/O devices. For example, touchscreen, monitors, headphones with mic, etc.

STORAGE DEVICES

A computer needs to store information for it to work. Hardware devices that are used to store data permanently or temporarily are called storage devices. We will now learn about these.

Hardware devices that are used to store data permanently or temporarily are called storage devices.

Hard Disk

A hard disk is used to store large amounts of data. If it is stored inside the CPU, it is called an **internal hard disk.** If it is present as a separate storage device, it is called an **external hard disk.**

Fig. 2.8 *Internal hard disk*

Fig. 2.9 *External hard disk*

Pen drive

A pen drive is used to transfer data from one computer to another. It is also known as **flash drive**. A pen drive is very small. You can carry it in your pocket.

Fig. 2.10 *Pen drive*

CD/DVD

A CD or a DVD is a circular disc that can store a lot of information. A computer can read from a CD or a DVD using the CD/DVD drive. A DVD can store more information than a CD.

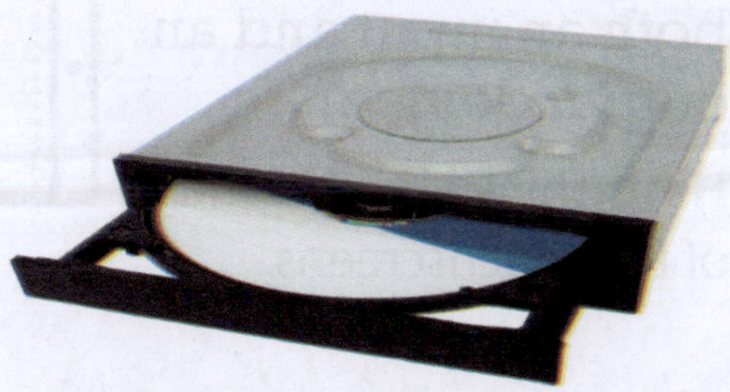

Fig. 2.11 *CD/DVD drive*

I am smart!

The full form of CD is Compact Disc and the full form of DVD is Digital Versatile Disc.

I can do!

Match the following.

a. Keyboard (i) 

b. Mouse (ii) 

c. CPU (iii) 

d. Pen drive (iv) 

e. Printer (v) 

What did I learn?

- Input is the information given to a computer.
- Processing is doing a certain task or action based on the input.
- Output is the information that the computer gives to the user after processing.
- A hardware device that provides input to the computer is called an input device. Keyboard, mouse, scanner, microphone, joystick and webcam are some input devices.

- A hardware device that shows the output to the user is called an output device. Monitor, speakers, printer, headphones, projector and plotter are some output devices.
- A hardware device that is used to store data is called a storage device. Some storage devices are hard disk, CD, DVD and pen drive.

Exercises

1. State whether the following statements are true (T) or false (F).

a. An input device is a device used to show the result to the user. ☐

b. Any information given to a computer for processing is called input. ☐

c. Printer and speakers are input devices. ☐

d. Computers process the input to give the output. ☐

e. Computers do not need input to work. ☐

2. Name the following devices.

a. 

b. 

c. 

d. 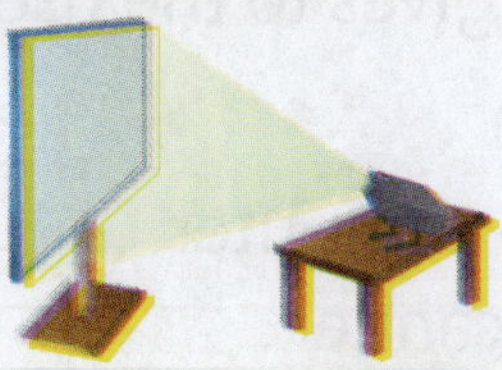

e. 

f. 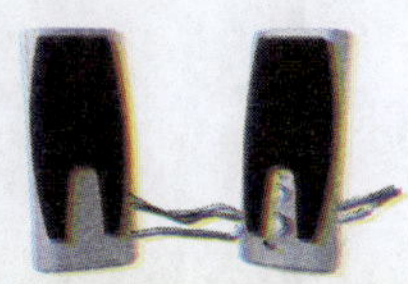

3. Look at the following pictures of devices. Rearrange the jumbled words and write their correct names in the blanks given.

a.  RDHA KSDI ____________________

b.  MWCEAB ____________________

c.  TTPLREO ____________________

d.  KSTJIOCY ____________________

e.  SHHEEAODNP ____________________

4. Fill in the blanks using the given words.

storage **CPU** **Input** **monitor** **output**

a. Processing of information happens in the ____________.

b. An ____________________ device shows the result to the user.

c. A ___________ is an example of an output device.

d. ____________________ is the information given by the user to the computer.

e. A hardware device used to store data permanently is called a ________ device.

5. Colour and label all the input devices in the picture.

Lab Activity

Look at a computer in your computer lab. Write the names of all the input and output devices you see there.

1. Input devices ______________________________

2. Output devices ______________________________

Think and Answer

Even our mobile phone is a computer. Can you think and tell which input device we use in our mobile phones?

____

____

____

____

3

Fun with MS Plaint

What will I learn?

- What is MS Paint?
- How can I use MS Paint to make my own drawings?
- What is the difference between Tux Paint and MS Paint?
- What is creativity?

Think and Discuss

Label the following types of computers and colour them.

In the previous class, we learnt about Tux Paint, which is used to make drawings on the computer. Now, we will explore a new application called Microsoft Paint.

OPENING MS PAINT

Microsoft (MS) Paint is a tool used to make drawings and colour them on the computer.

To open MS Paint, follow the steps given below:

1. Click on the **Start** button and type 'MS Paint' in the Search bar on the bottom-left corner.
2. Click on the **MS Paint** option. The home screen of MS Paint appears (Fig. 3.1).

Fig. 3.1 *Home screen of MS Paint*

Parts of MS Paint Window

The Paint window opens with the **File** tab selected. Figure 3.2 shows the basic parts of the Paint window.

I am smart!

When we open the Paint program, the name of the file is '*Untitled*', until we give it a new name.

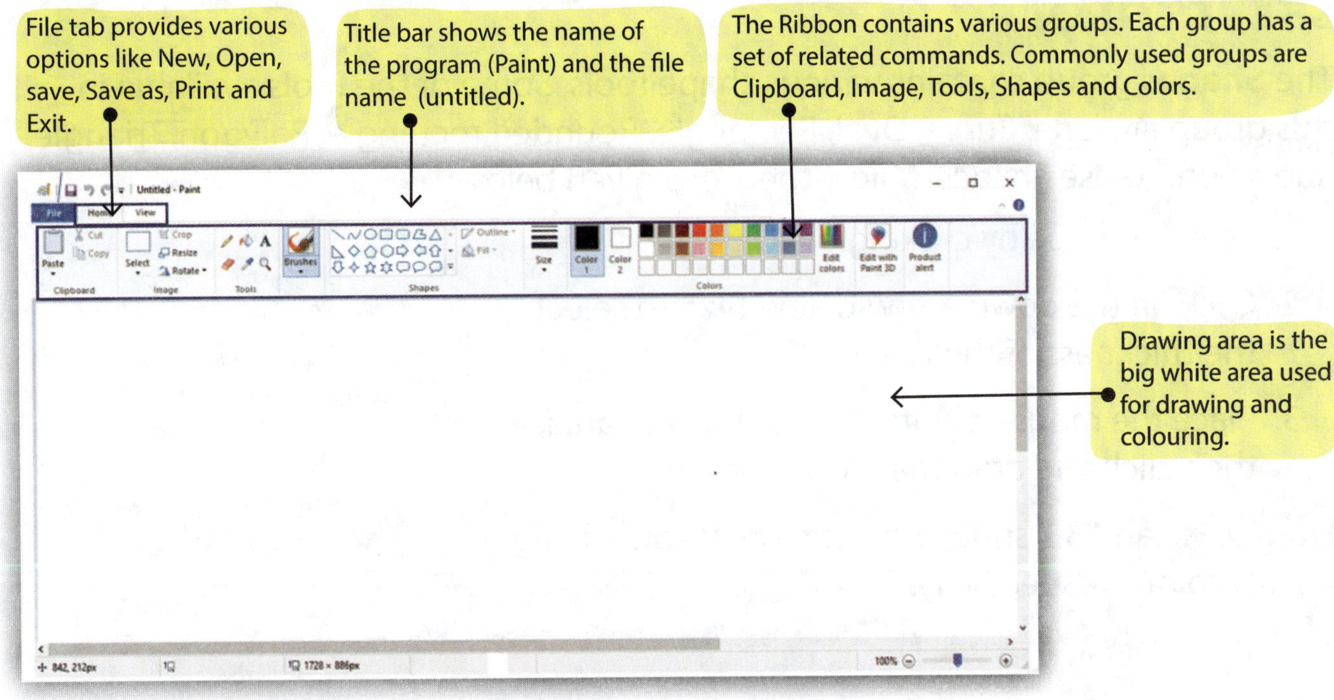

Fig. 3.2 *Home screen of MS Paint*

Let us discuss these parts in detail.

COLORS GROUP

Fig. 3.3 *Colors palette*

To choose the colours with which we want to paint, we use the **Colors** group. There are 20 colours in the Colors palette that can be used to colour a drawing.

The **Edit Colors** option helps select any shade of a colour. When we select this option, a dialog box appears, as shown in Fig. 3.4. After selecting your favourite colour, click on the **OK** button.

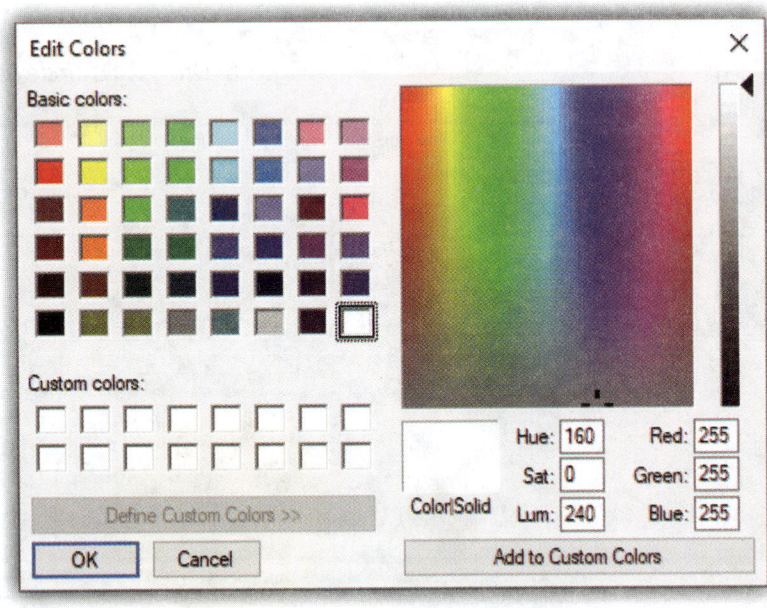

Fig. 3.4 *Edit Colors dialog box*

Color 1 and Color 2

We can select a foreground colour by clicking on **Color 1** in the **Colors** group and then choosing a colour. We can also select a background colour by clicking on **Color 2** and then choosing a colour.

SHAPES GROUP

The **Shapes** group contains various shape tools. Some of the tools available in this group are Line, Curve, Oval, Rectangle, Rounded rectangle, Polygon, Triangle, and so on. To use Shapes, follow the steps given below:

1. Select a shape by clicking on it.
2. Click on the down arrow below **Size** to select the thickness of the line.
3. Place the mouse pointer in the drawing area, then click and drag the mouse pointer.

Fig. 3.5 *Shapes*

Figures 3.6 and 3.7 show drawing a circle and filling it with colour, respectively.

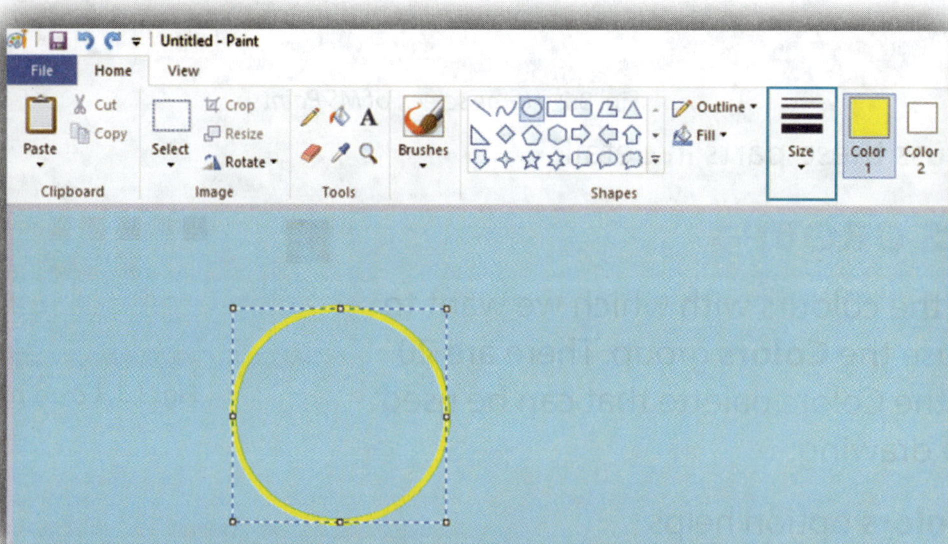

Fig. 3.6 *Drawing a circle using Shapes*

Fig. 3.7 *Colouring the circle using the Fill with color tool*

I can do!

Colour the clown as per the colours given for each shape. Can you draw the same using MS Paint?

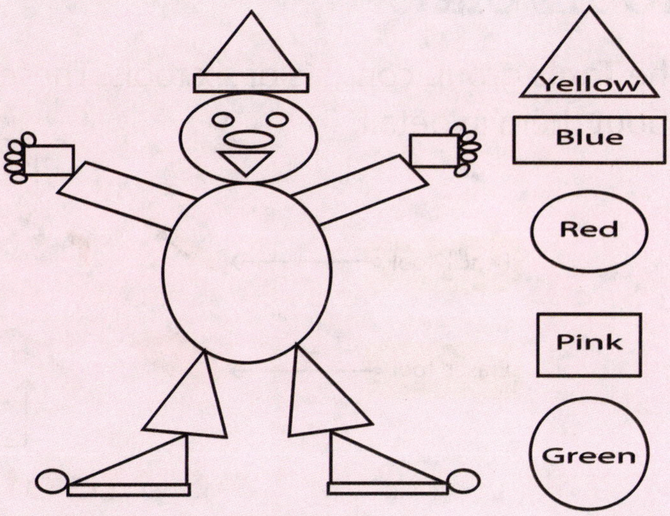

BRUSHES

We use brushes to draw lines and curves. There are different kinds of brushes. They can be used to draw lines of different styles and textures.

1. Select the **Brushes** tool from the **Tools** group. The small arrow under **Brushes** allows us to select different types of brushes (Fig. 3.8).
2. Click on the down arrow below **Size** to select the thickness of the brush.
3. Select a foreground colour by clicking on **Color 1** in the **Colors** group.
4. Select a background colour by clicking on **Color 2**.
5. To paint a picture using the selected brush, click and drag the mouse inside the drawing area.

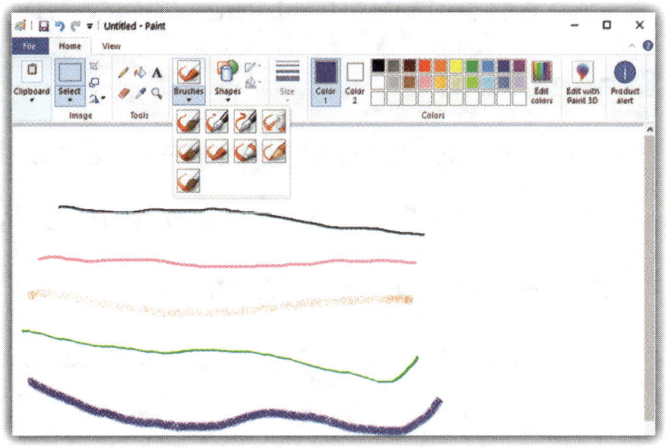

Fig. 3.8 *Brushes tool*

I can do!

Open the Paint program. Select the Brushes tool. Write your name using different brushes and colours.

TOOLS GROUP

The **Tools** group consists of six tools. These tools are discussed below. Let us learn about them in detail.

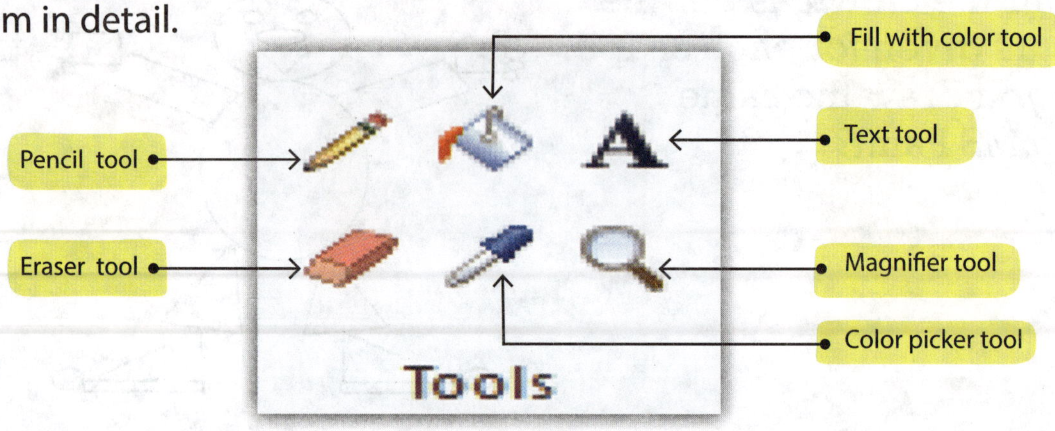

Fig. 3.9 *Tools group*

Pencil Tool

The **Pencil** tool is used to draw any shape, just like a real pencil. To use this tool:

1. Select the **Pencil** from the **Tools** group.
2. Click on the arrow below **Size** to select the thickness of the line.
3. Select the colour of your choice from **Colors** group.

Eraser Tool

The **Eraser** tool is used to erase a part or the entire drawing. To use this tool:

1. Select the **Eraser** tool from the Tools group.
2. Select the size of the eraser.
3. Click and drag the mouse pointer over the parts of the image you want to erase.

Color Picker Tool

The **Color picker** tool is used to copy colour from one part of the picture and fill another part with the same colour. To use this tool:

1. Click on the **Color picker** tool from the **Tools** group.
2. Click on the part of the picture from where you want to pick the colour. The picked-up colour will be reflected as **Color 1**.
3. Move the mouse pointer to the part of the picture where you want to apply the same colour. Then, click on it once to apply the same colour.

Fill with Color Tool

The **Fill with color** tool is used to colour the background or a shape. For filling colour:

1. Select the **Fill with color** tool from the **Tools** group.
2. Pick a colour after clicking on **Color 1**.
3. Click inside the shape you want to fill with colour.

Text Tool

The **Text** tool is used to write on the drawing. It has various options for different styles of letters, colours and sizes. To use this tool:

1. Click on the **Text** tool.
2. Click on the place in the drawing where the text needs to be placed.
3. Write the desired text.

Magnifier Tool

To magnify or zoom in different parts of the picture, we use the **Magnifier** tool. To use this tool:

1. Click on the **Magnifier** tool.
2. Move the mouse on the part of the image you want to magnify.

I can do!

1. Open MS Paint and write the following sentence on a green background.

Nature is beautiful!

Try the B, I, U options and see what they do.

2. Draw a Rainbow using the different tools. Write names of colours used to draw it.

DIFFERENCE BETWEEN TUX PAINT AND MS PAINT

Both Tux Paint and MS Paint are used for drawing and colouring on the computer. However, there are some ways in which they are different from each other.

Tux Paint	MS Paint
1. It has a mascot named Tux.	It has no mascot.
2. It has no tool to fill colour in shapes.	The Fill with color tool can be used to fill colours.
3. It does not allow us to make custom colours.	It allows us to make custom colours.
4. It has different backgrounds to choose from.	It has only a white background.

CREATIVITY

Dan's friends Aman and Veer came to his house. After playing for hours together, all of them decided to make drawings with their new crayons. They decided to draw a scenery with a house. After they finished, they saw each other's scenery. Their drawings are shown in Fig. 3.10.

Dan

Aman

Veer

Fig. 3.10 *Different drawings of sceneries with houses*

Creativity is the use of imagination to make something new.

All of them had to draw a scenery with a house. As their imaginations were different, they created drawings that looked different from each other.

Creativity is not limited to drawings. There are several ways in which one can be creative.

Buildings

Poems

3D printing

Stories

Fig. 3.11 *Various kinds of creativity*

I can do!

Can you draw a scenery with a house on a computer? If yes, list the tools and shapes from MS Paint you will use to draw this.

....

....

I can do!

Open the Paint program. Select the Text tool. Write your name using different font styles and colours.

What did I learn?

- MS Paint is used to draw and paint on the computer.
- MS Paint drawings, when saved, are stored as images.
- To choose the colours with which we want to paint, we use the Colors palette.
- The Shapes group contains various shapes like line, curve, oval, rectangle, rounded rectangle, polygon, triangle, etc.
- The Brushes tool can be used to draw lines of different styles and textures.
- The Pencil tool is used to draw any shape, just like a real pencil.
- The fill with color tool is used to colour the background or a shape.
- The Text tool is used to write on the drawing.
- The Eraser tool is used to erase a part or the entire drawing.
- The Color picker tool is used to copy colour from one part of the picture and fill another part with the same colour.
- To magnify or zoom in different parts of the picture, we use the Magnifier tool.
- Creativity is the use of imagination to make something new.
- Creativity is not limited to drawings. There are several ways in which one can be creative.

Exercises

1. Fill in the blanks using the given words.

six **Brushes** **Edit Colors** **File** **pictures**

a. MS Paint is used to draw and colour ________________ on the computers.

b. The Tools group consists of ________________ tools.

c. We use ________________ tool to draw lines and curves.

d. The ________________ option helps select any shade of a colour.

e. The Paint window opens with the ________________ tab selected.

2. Write the names of the tab, group and tool used to perform the following tasks.

S. No.	Task	Tab	Group	Tool
a.	Writing name in a picture			
b.	Writing name in a picture			
c.	Writing your names using a brush			
d.	Inserting a rectangle in the drawing area			

3. Answer the following questions in one word.

a. Name the tool used to draw different shapes. ________________

b. Which tool will you use to draw a straight line? ________________

c. Name the tool used to erase a part of drawing. ________________

d. Which group helps you to colour the shape? ________________

e. What do you call the area which is used for drawing and colouring?

____

Lab Activity

1. Try using the following tools in MS Paint and write down what they do.

 Zoom in	
 Zoom out	

2. Using the Shapes group, draw the following shapes and fill them with the colours of your choice.

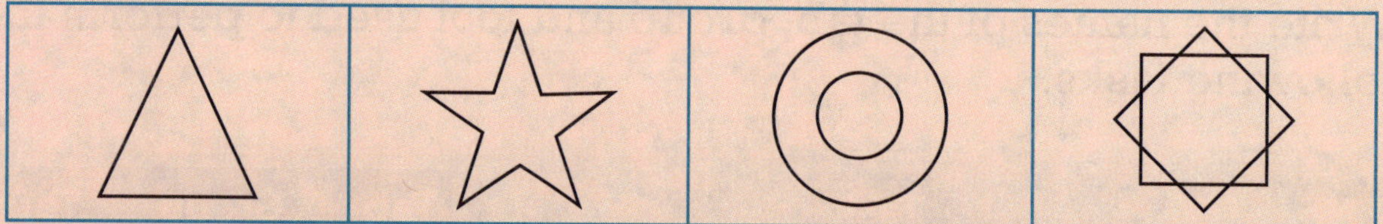

3. Draw the following pictures with the help of the Pencil tool.

   a. Clouds

   b. Moon and stars

   c. Leaf

   d. Butterfly

4. Draw the following using Pencil and/or Shapes tools and write the text given here with it.

Drawing	**Text**
Flower	'Name of the flower'
Tree	'Protect trees'
Kite	'Let us fly kites today!'
Mango	'The yellow fruit.'

4

Exploring MS Paint

What will I learn?

- How to select a picture?
- What is the use of the Clipboard group?
- How can I crop, rotate and resize an image?

Think and Discuss

In the previous chapter, we have learnt how to use MS Paint to draw and colour on the computer. MS Paint files are saved as images. But, what happens after we save the images? What can we do with them?

Look at the following pictures. Fill in the blanks using the given words.

email **print** **show**

a. We can ________ pictures to our teachers.

b. We can __________ pictures to our friends.

c. We can __________ pictures to make a photo album.

SELECTING AN IMAGE

Sometimes, we need to move a part of the drawing or move the text from one part to another. The **Select** tool is used to select the entire drawing or a part of it.

To select the entire drawing, follow the steps given below:

1. Click on the **Select** tool drop-down arrow from the **Image** group of the **Home** tab.
2. The drop-down menu shows two selection shapes, named **Rectangular selection** and **Free-form selection**. Based on the shape selected, the **Select** tool gives us various options to choose from.

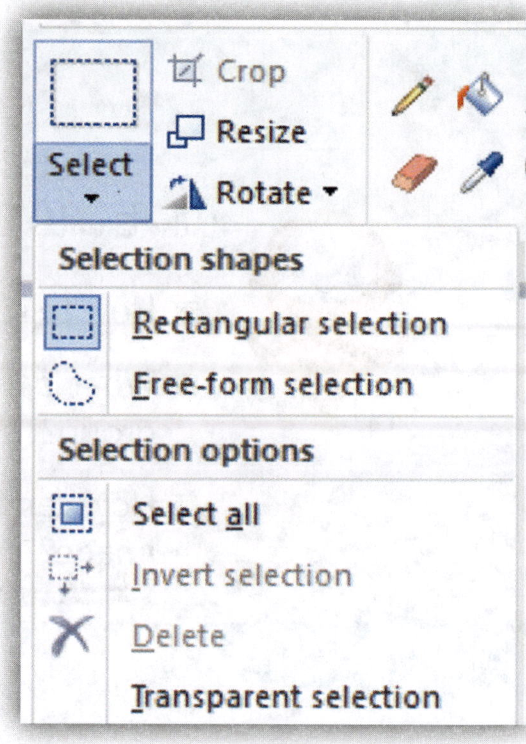

Fig. 4.1 *Select tool drop-down menu*

Rectangular selection: This option is used to select a rectangular or square area of the image.

Free-form selection: It allows us to select an object of any shape by dragging the mouse around the shape.

Fig. 4.2 *Selecting part of an image*

I can tell!

Under the **Select** tool, there are four more options. These are: Select all, Invert selection, Delete and Transparent selection. Explore these and write down what they do.

CLIPBOARD GROUP

The **Clipboard** group is present under the **Home** tab of the MS Paint application. It consists of three tools: Cut, Copy and Paste (Fig. 4.3).

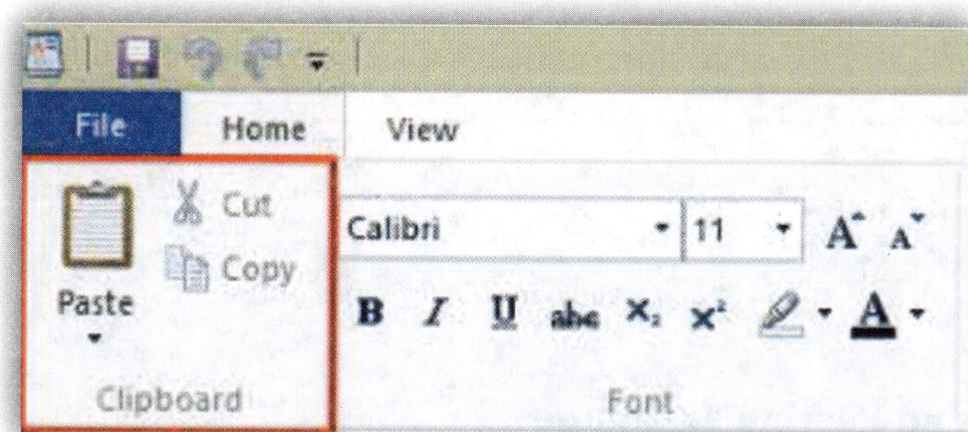

Fig. 4.3 *Clipboard group*

Cutting and Pasting an Image

The **Cut** option takes out the selection which can then be pasted. To cut a picture or a part of it and paste it in another part of the picture, follow the steps given below:

1. Select the part of the drawing you want to cut by using the **Select** tool in the **Image** group.

2. Click on the **Cut** option in the **Clipboard** group.
3. Click on the **Paste** option in the **Clipboard** group.
4. With the picture still selected, move it to a new place in the Drawing Area.

Fig. 4.4 *Cutting and pasting an image*

Copying and Pasting an Image

The copy option makes a copy of the selection, which can then be pasted. To copy a picture or a part of it and paste it in another part of the picture, follow the steps given below:

1. Select the part of the drawing you want to copy by using the **Select** tool in the **Image** group.
2. Click on the **Copy** option in the **Clipboard** group.
3. Click on the **Paste** option in the **Clipboard** group.
4. With the picture still selected, move it to a new place in the Drawing Area.

Fig. 4.5 *Copying and pasting an image*

Knowledge Bytes

The cut/copied part of the picture is stored in a temporary folder called Clipboard.

I am smart!

To select the entire picture: Ctrl+A
To cut a part of the picture: Ctrl+X
To copy a part of the picture: Ctrl+C
To paste the cut/copied part of the picture: Ctrl+V

I can do!

Draw two yellow circles in MS Paint. Copy these circles and paste on the drawing area. Now, using the **Selection** tool, select the second one and change its colour, as shown below.

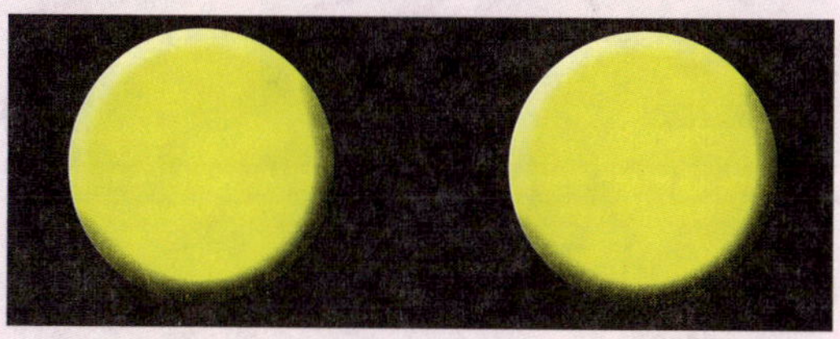

IMAGE GROUP

The **Image** group consists of four tools: Select, Crop, Rotate and Resize. We have learnt how to use the **Select** tool. Let us discuss other tools in detail.

> **Knowledge Bytes**
>
> Cropped images from one drawing can be copied and pasted in another drawing.

Cropping an Image

The **Crop tool** is used to select an area of the picture and cut out everything outside this area.

To use this tool, follow the steps given below:

1. Using the **Select** tool, select the part of the image you want to keep.

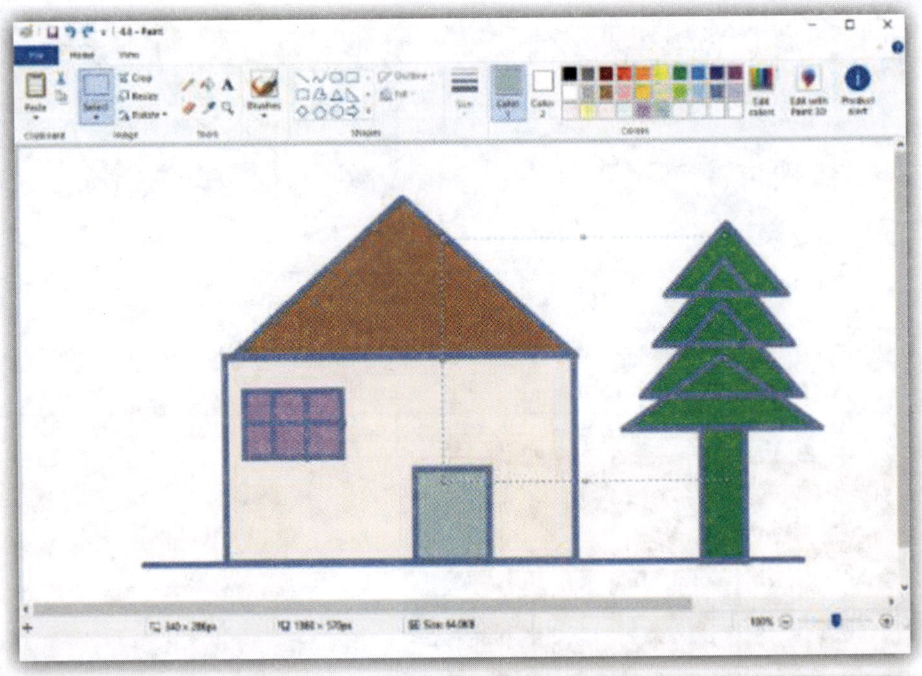

2. Click on the **Crop** tool in the Image group. You will see that only the cropped part of the image is there on the drawing area (Fig. 4.6).

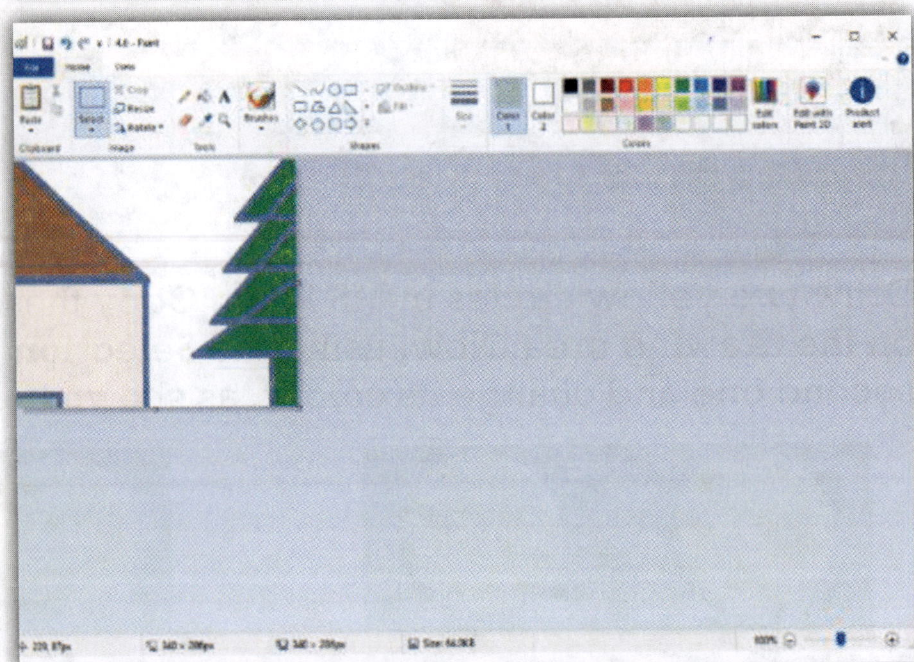

Fig. 4.6 *Using the Crop tool*

Rotating an Image

Rotate is used to turn the image to point in any direction, such as up, down, left or right. To use the **Rotate** tool, select the picture, then click on the **Rotate** tool in the **Image** group, and then, select the desired option.

I am smart!

Draw an image of a bird in MS Paint. Now, explore the various options under Rotate.

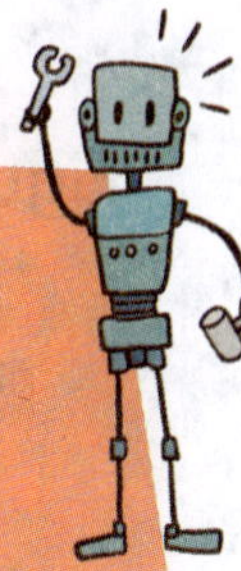

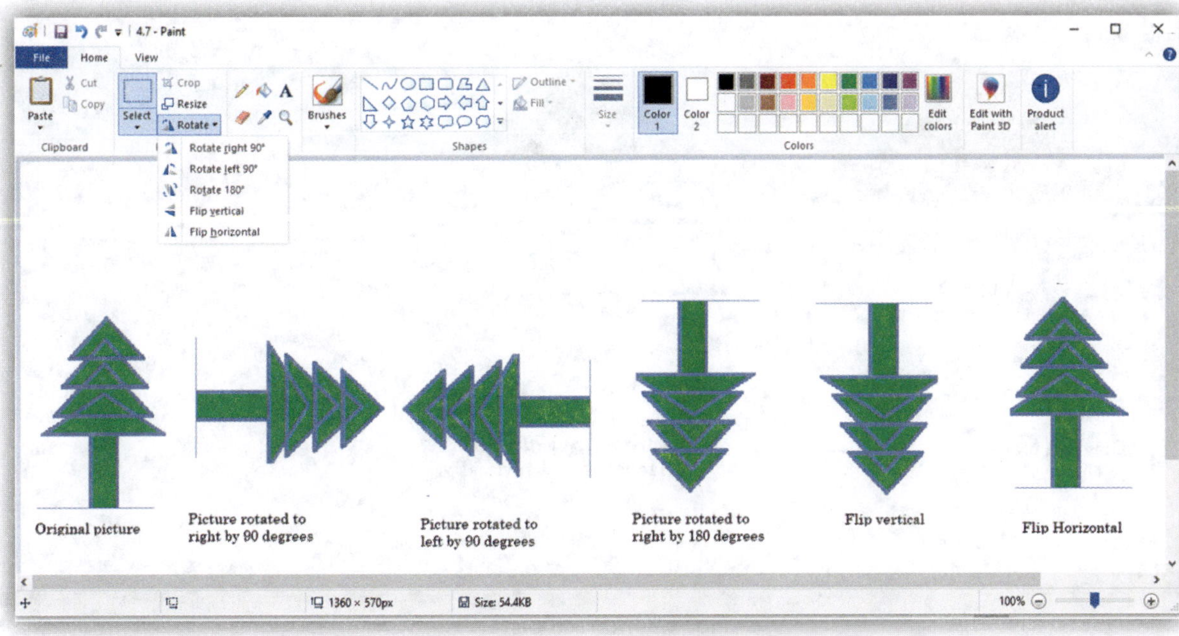

Fig. 4.7 *Using the Rotate tool*

Resizing the Image

As the name suggests, the **Resize** tool is used to make the image smaller or bigger. When we click on this tool, the **Resize and Skew** dialog box opens up, as shown in Fig. 4.8. It gives us options to resize and skew the image.

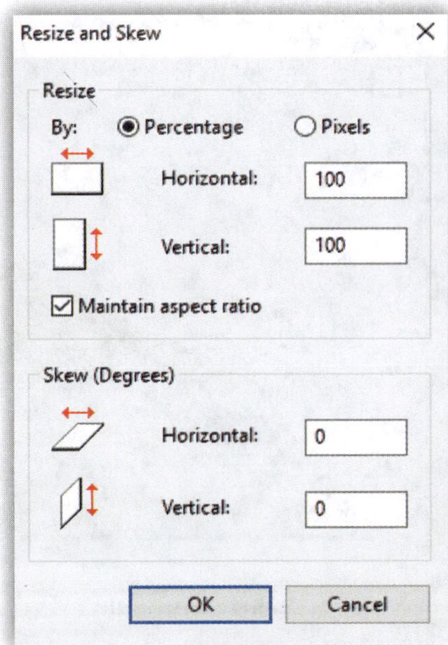

Fig. 4.8 *Resize and Skew dialog box*

The image can be resized by:

- **Percentage**: This is used to resize the image in relation to the current size which is 100%. Any value less than 100 decreases the size of the image while any value more than 100 increases the size of the image.
- **Pixel**: Pixel is a way to measure the exact size of the image. Changing the pixel values, changes the size of the image as well.

Figure 4.9 shows a resized picture.

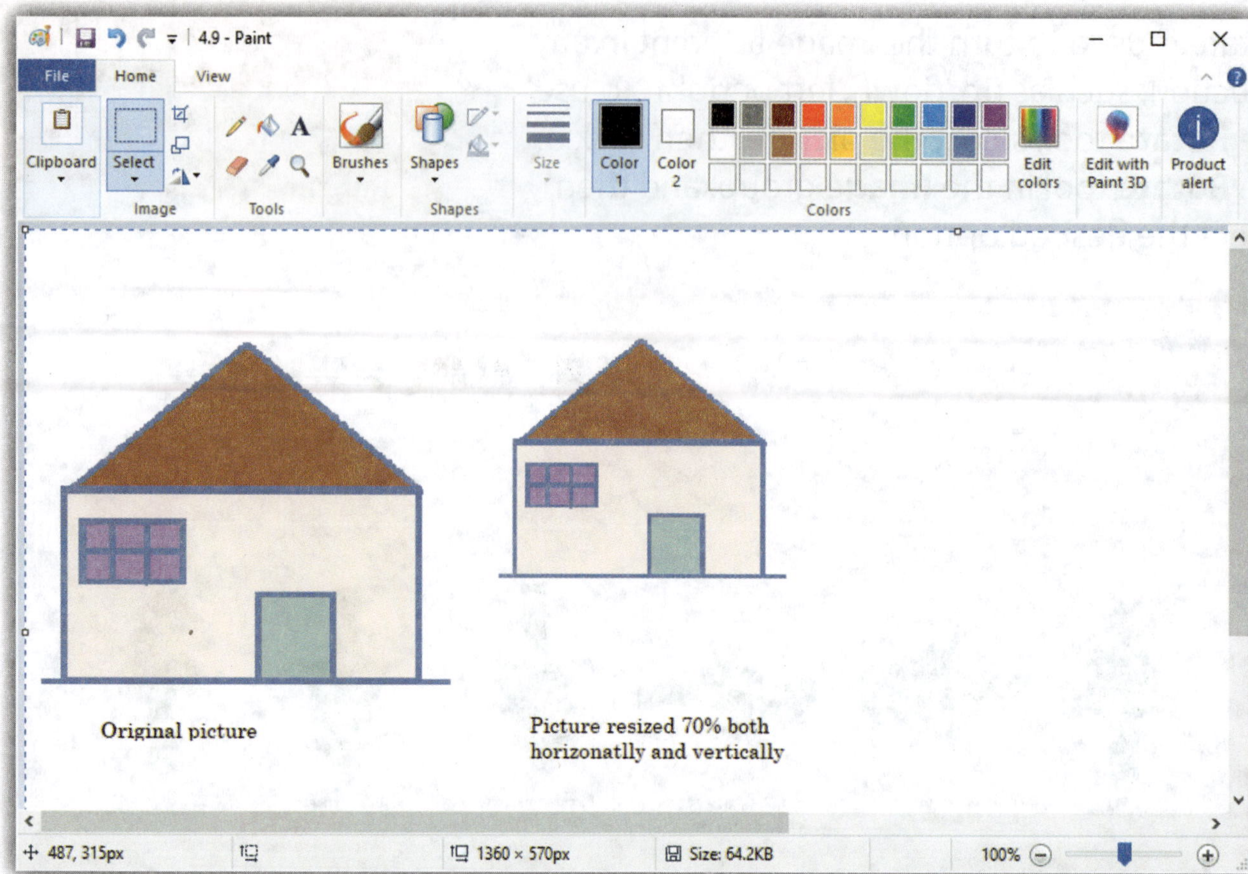

Fig. 4.9 *Resized picture*

Similarly, to skew (tilt) the image, enter the numbers in the Horizontal and Vertical boxes (Fig. 4.10).

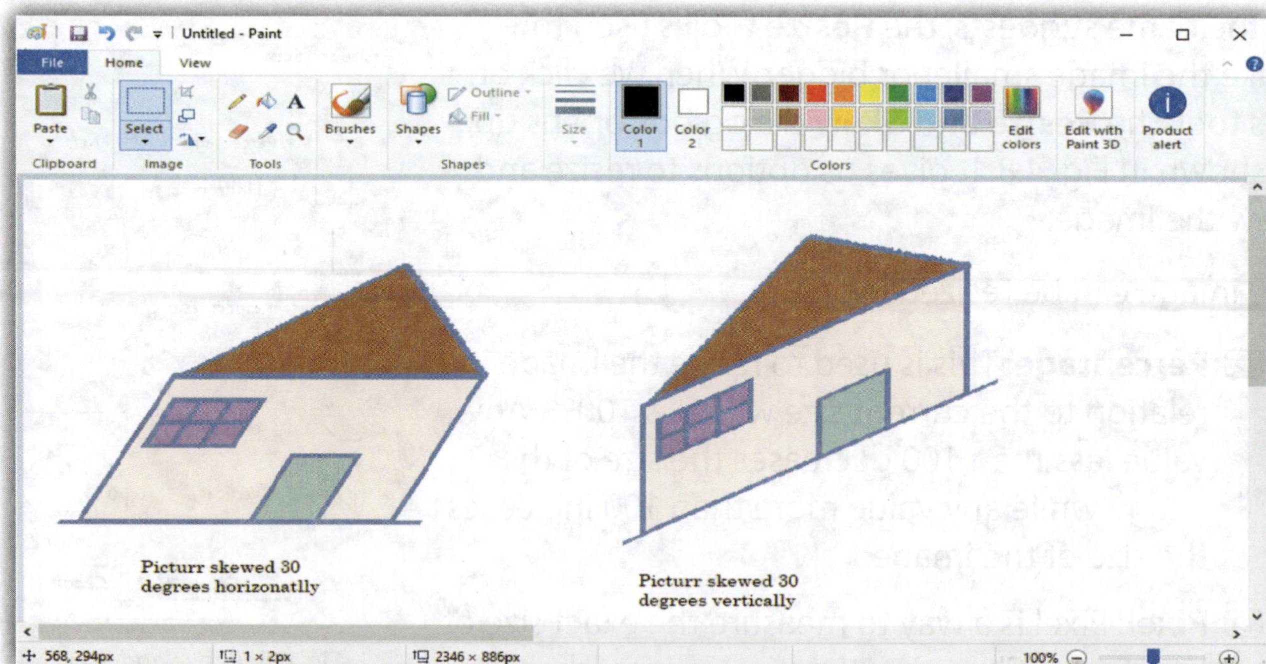

Fig. 4.10 *Skewed pictures*

I can do!

Draw a smiley in MS Paint. Now, explore the various options available in the Image group, such as Crop, Resize and Rotate.

I am smart!

To crop a picture: Ctrl+Shift+X

To resize and skew the picture: Ctrl+W

MORE ON THE TEXT TOOL A

We have already learnt about the **Text** tool. It is used to add text to an image. To add text to the image, follow the steps given below:

1. Under the **Home** tab, in the **Tools** group, click on the **Text** tool (Fig. 4.11).

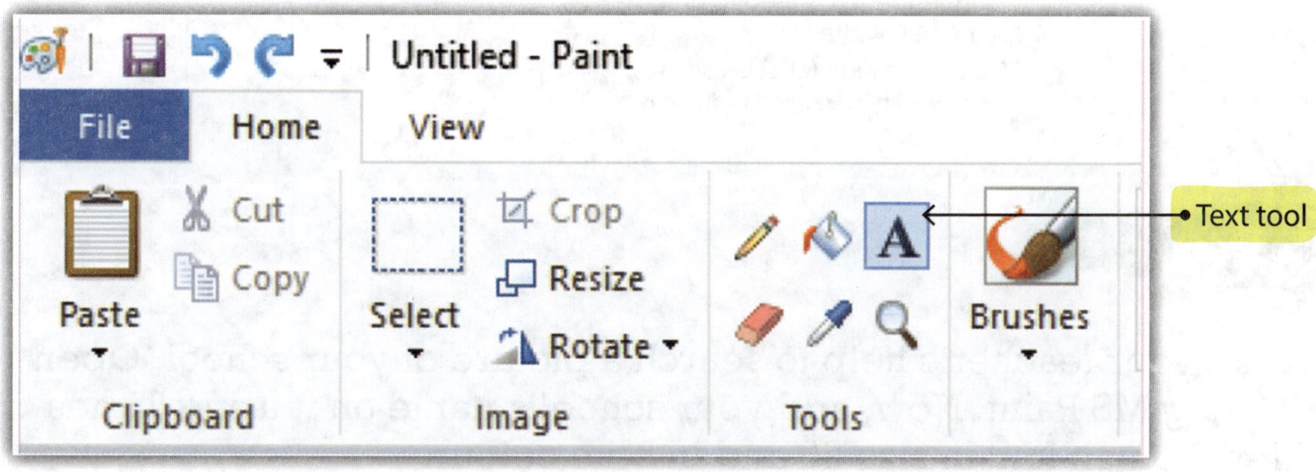

Fig. 4.11 *Text tool*

2. Drag the pointer to the drawing area where text needs to be added. Notice that the **Text** tab appears on the Paint window (Fig. 4.12).
3. From the **Text** tab, in the **Font** group, select the font face, size and style.
4. In the **Colors** group, click **Color 1**, choose the desired text colour and start typing the text.

Font is similar to handwriting. We can select the different types of font styles from here.

Opaque and Transparent indicate the background of the text selection.

Colors group is used to select the colour of the text, as well as its background.

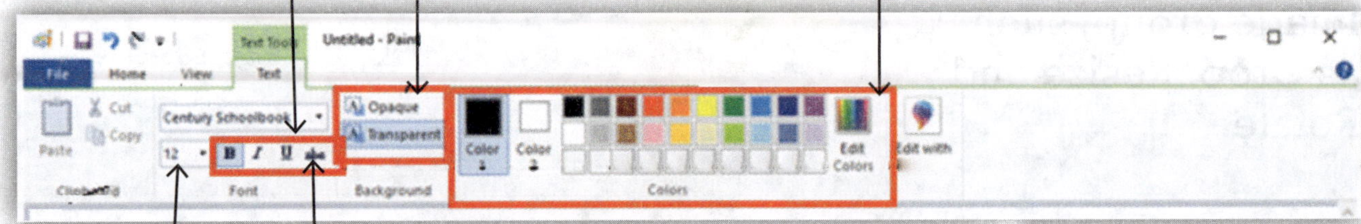

Font size changes the size of the text.

Bold (**B**) is used to make the text appear **bold** (thicker).

Italic (*I*) is used to make the text slant to the right.

Underline (U) is used to draw a line below the text.

Strikethrough (~~abc~~) is used to draw a line ~~over the text~~.

Fig. 4.12 *Text tab*

I can do!

Take your teacher's help to search a picture of your school. Open it using MS Paint. Now, add your school's name on it using Times New Roman font in size 20 and in blue colour.

Knowledge Bytes

MS Paint is used for 2D drawing. It allows us to create 3D drawing as well. When we click on the Edit with Paint 3D option on the MS Paint window, a new window appears, which allows us to create 3D paintings.

What did I learn?

- Rectangular selection is used to select a square or a rectangular part of the picture.
- Free-form selection is used to select an irregularly shaped part of the picture.
- Cut and Paste commands are used to remove or delete a picture or part of a picture and paste it in another place on the drawing area.
- Copy and Paste options are used to duplicate or copy a picture or part of a picture and paste it in another place on the drawing area.
- The Crop tool is used to select an area of the picture and cut out everything outside this area.
- The Rotate tool is used to rotate or flip a picture or part of a picture.
- The Resize tool is used to resize or skew a picture or part of a picture.
- The Text tool is used to type text.

Exercises

1. Fill in the blanks using the given words.

Font size　Resize　Ctrl+A　Select　draw

a. MS Paint is an application used to _________ on the computer.

b. The _________ tool is used to select a part of a picture.

c. We can change the size of the text by using the _________ option.

d. To change the size of the image, we use the _________ tool.

e. _________ is the keyboard shortcut for selecting the entire image.

2. Match the following.

a.		(i) Crop
b.		(ii) Paste
c.		(iii) Select
d.		(iv) Rotate

3. Write the keyboard shortcuts for the following commands.

a. Cut

b. Copy

c. Paste

d. Select All

e. Crop

f. Resize and Skew

4. Answer the following questions in one word.

a. Name the tool used to turn an image upside down. ____________________

b. Which tool will you use to cut out one portion of a drawing?
____

c. Name the tool used to select the entire drawing. ____________________

d. Which option will you use to increase the size of the text? ____________________

Lab Activity

1. Draw the following pictures by using the various tools in MS Paint.

   a. Cricket bat

   b. Leaf

   c. Ice cream

   d. Your favourite vegetable

2. Look at the following picture of seven days of the week. Choose a day of your choice and paste (draw) it in the blank area. Colour the day using the your favourite colours. Can you do this in MS Paint? Name the tools you will be using for this.

3. Guess the names of the following board games. Now, using the Text tool, write their names in MS Paint in the styles given below.

S. No.	Image	Font Style	Font Colour
a.		Calibri, Size: 30, Bold, Underline and Transparent	Brown
b.		Comic Sans MS, Size: 45, Bold, Underline, Opaque with white background	Purple

4. Sameer and Rima decided to draw a scenery by dividing it in to two parts. Now, they are unable to join both the drawings together to make it into a big scenery. Which MS Paint tools should they use for it?

5 Fun with Patterns

What will I learn?

- What is step-by-step thinking?
- What are sequences and patterns?

Think and Discuss

Raja comes home from the park. He is very thirsty. He wants to drink water. His mother has gone to the market. His father is busy on the phone. Look at the pictures below. They show the steps that Raja needs to follow to get water. Number them to show the order of steps he should follow.

Keeps it on the table

Takes a glass from the shelf

Drinks water

Goes to the kitchen

Carefully pours water from the jug into the glass

Climbs on a chair

Like Raja, we all follow many steps every day to do our work, have fun, etc. Some times, we follow the steps without thinking. Sometimes, we have to remember the steps and follow them carefully.

STEP-BY-STEP THINKING

To do any work, we have to follow a set of steps. Some tasks are simple. They can be performed in a few steps. Other tasks are difficult. To do such tasks, we need to think about each step and the order of the steps too. This is called step-by-step or sequential thinking.

Step-by-step thinking means to think and act in an orderly manner.

I can do!

Raja's brother Ravi is very lazy. Here are the steps that Raja and Ravi follow to reach school.

Raja	Ravi
1. Wake up	1. Wake up
2. Brush my teeth	2. Rinse my mouth
3. Rinse my mouth	3. Brush my teeth
4. Take bath	4. Have breakfast
5. Wear school uniform	5. Wear school uniform
6. Have breakfast	6. Take bath
7. Go to school	7. Go to school

1. Who do you think reaches school on time?

....

2. What should Ravi do to reach school on time?

....

3. What steps do you follow to reach school on time?

....

SEQUENCES AND PATTERNS

We see many shapes around us. They are everywhere. Some times, they appear in a fixed order. A particular order in which related things follow each other is called a sequence for example, the sequence of letters, numbers, shapes, etc.

Shapes can also be put together in an order to form sequences.

Fig. 5.1 *Various shapes*

> A particular order in which related things follow each other is called sequence.

Here are some examples of designs we see around us.

Triangles in our party decoration

Squares and colours in our clothes

Rectangles on the floor

Fig. 5.2 *Designs around us*

Designs formed by repeating colours, objects and shapes are called patterns. Here are a few patterns.

Designs formed by repeating colours, objects and shapes are called patterns.

Fig. 5.3 *Different patterns*

design: the process and art of planning and making a detailed drawing of something

I can do!

Draw the repeated pattern used to create different images shown in Fig. 5.3.

I can tell!

1. Look at the following pictures carefully. Tick (✓) the picture if it shows a pattern.

a.

b.

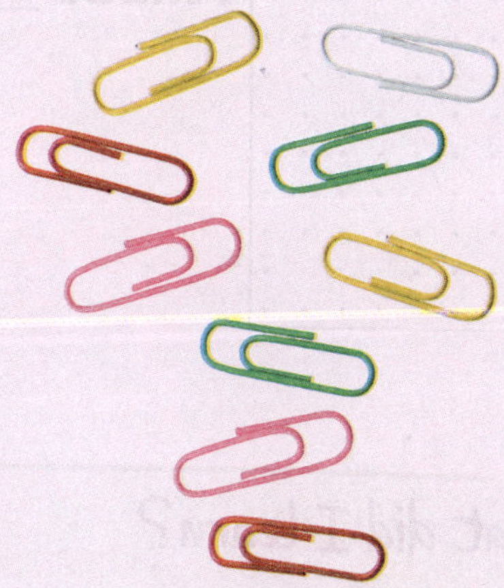

c.

d.

2. Do you see patterns around you? If yes, write their names.

....

....

....

I can do!

Connect the dots to make as many shapes as you can. Write your answer in the space given.

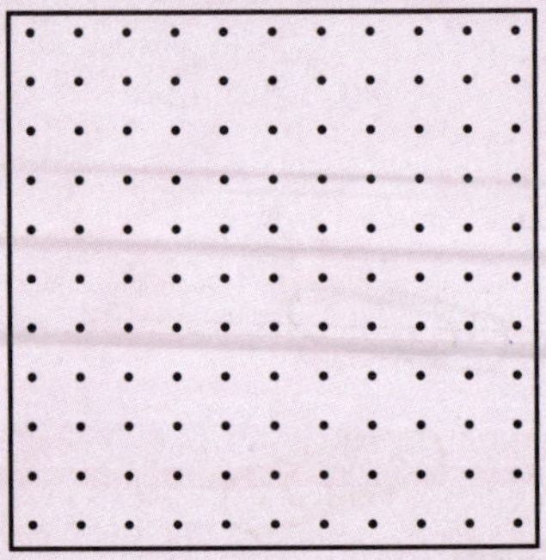

I made ______ shapes by connecting the dots.

What did I learn?

- Step-by-step thinking means to think and act in an orderly manner.
- A particular order in which related things follow each other is called a sequence.
- Designs formed by repeating shapes, colours and objects are called patterns.

Exercises

1. Here are the steps to write your name inside a new notebook. Which step is not in order? Write the correct order of steps.

a. Open the notebook.

b. Close the notebook.

c. Write your name.

d. Take the pencil from the pencil box.

2. **We should always wash our hands with soap before eating. Fill in the blanks to complete the steps that we should follow.**

a. Wet our hands.

b. Apply ______________________.

c. Rub the hands to clean them.

d. Rinse with water.

e. Wipe with a clean ____________.

3. **Rina is playing in the playground. Write the order of the steps followed by Rina.**

a. Slide down happily.

b. Climb the ladder.

c. Wait for her turn.

4. It is very important to keep things in their place. We can find them easily the next time we want. Here are the steps you should follow to draw and colour pictures in your drawing book. Look at the pictures and fill in the blanks to complete the steps.

a. Take the colours from the table.

b. Take out your drawing book from the shelf.

c. Draw and colour your favourite things.

d. Put the _____ back on the table.

e. Put the ____________________ back in the shelf.

5. Check if the following sequences are correct. If not, write the correct sequences in the given space.

a. A B D C ____________________

b. M O N P ____________________

c. 4 5 7 6 9 8 10 11 ____________________

d. 5 4 2 3 1 ____________________

6. The following sequences are incomplete. Fill in the missing letters/numbers to complete these.

a. 1 2 3 ☐☐

b. S T U V ☐☐

c. 1 3 5 7 ☐☐

d. 2 4 6 ☐☐

e. J K L M ☐☐ P

7. Identify the pattern in the following pictures. Draw and colour the missing shapes in the given space.

a.

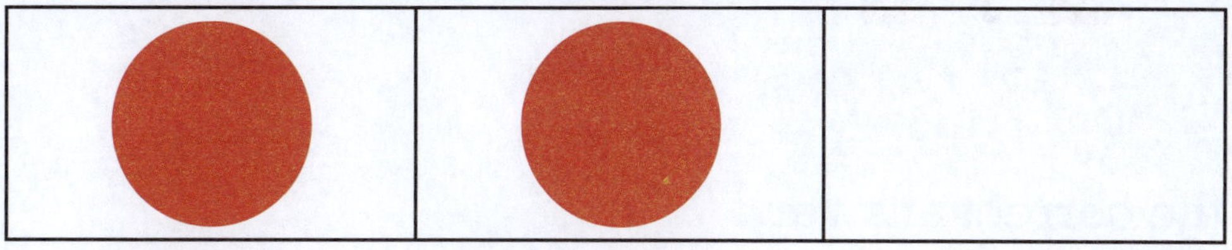

b

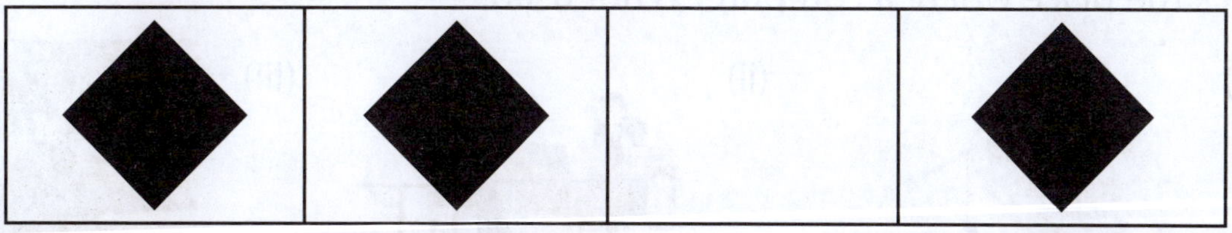

c

d.

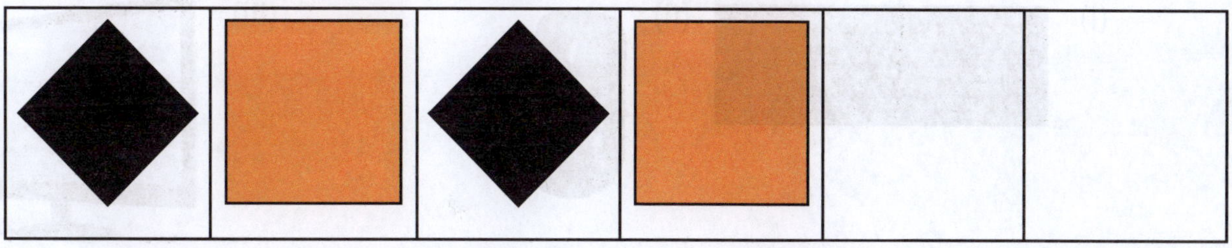

e.

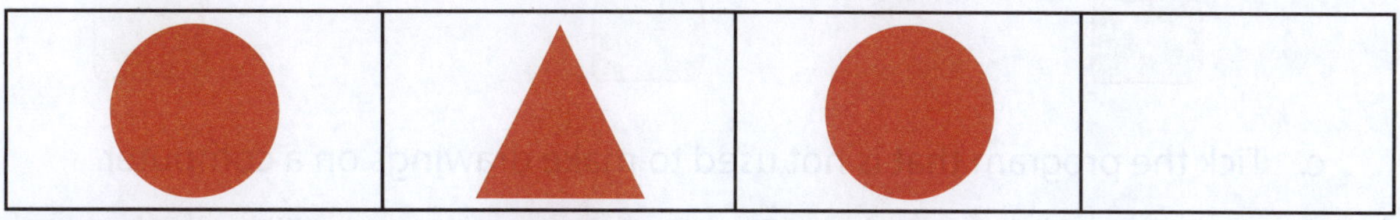

f.

g.

Worksheet 1

1. Tick (✓) the correct answer.

a. Tick the place where a computer is not used.

(i) 

(ii) 

(iii) 

b. Tick the output device.

(i) 

(ii) 

(iii) 

c. Tick the program that is not used to make drawings on a computer.

(i) 

(ii) 

(iii) 

d. Tick the picture of a storage device.

(i)

(ii)

(iii)

e. Tick the option you will use to insert shapes in a drawing.

(i)

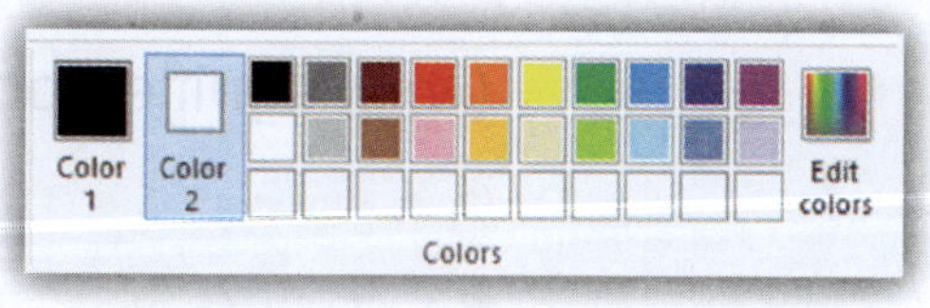

(ii)

(iii)

2. Fill in the blanks using the given words.

computer output CPU Software Input

a. Headphone is an ______________ device.

b. ______________ is a set of instructions that tell the computer how to work.

c. ______________ is known as the brain of the computer.

d. MS Paint is used to create drawings on a ______________.

e. Microphone is an ______________ device.

3. Match the following.

a.		(i) Fill with color tool
b.		(ii) Brushes tool
c.		(iii) Color picker tool
d.		(iv) Magnifier tool
e.		(v) Text tool

4. Find the following words in the grid given below.

Hardware Computer Software Input Output Storage

O	E	M	O	S	S	L	L	M
U	M	W	A	H	O	S	S	O
T	A	M	E	A	F	T	T	U
P	I	N	P	U	T	T	O	R
U	H	A	R	D	W	A	R	E
T	T	I	I	S	A	O	A	E
H	W	L	L	E	R	E	G	S
J	X	E	B	L	E	T	E	K
M	C	O	M	P	U	T	E	R

5. In the following image of the keyboard, colour the number keys **red**, the arrow keys **green**, the letter keys **blue** and the function keys **yellow**.

Projects

1. Collect pictures of places where you have seen a computer being used. Paste these on your notebook.
2. Draw a picture of the rainbow. Also, write the names of all the colours used to create it.

Worksheet 2

1. Fill in the blanks using the given words.

Rotate **sequence** **Rectangular** **Patterns** **Clipboard**

a. ____________ is a selection tool in MS Paint.

b. Cut option is present under the ____________ group in MS Paint.

c. ____________ are regularly repeating designs.

d. The next letter in the ________________ P, Q, R, S is T.

e. ____________ tool is present under the Image group in MS Paint.

2. State whether the following statements are true (T) or false (F).

a. The Rotate tool is used to make an image smaller or bigger. ☐

b. Pixel is the way to measure the exact size of an image. ☐

c. The Clipboard group is present on the Home tab of the MS Paint application. ☐

d. 1, 2, 3, 4, 5 represents a pattern. ☐

e. Font size changes the size of the image. ☐

3. Look at the pictures of Paint tools. Rearrange the jumbled words and write their names in the given space.

a.  IRZEES ____________________

b.  TTROEA ____________________

c.  YPOC ____________________

d.  ETTX ____________________

e.  TPAES ____________________

4. Colour the following shapes in such a way that they make a pattern.

a.

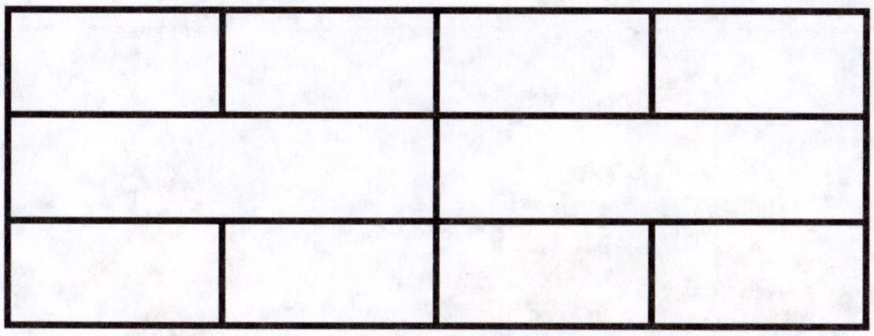

b.

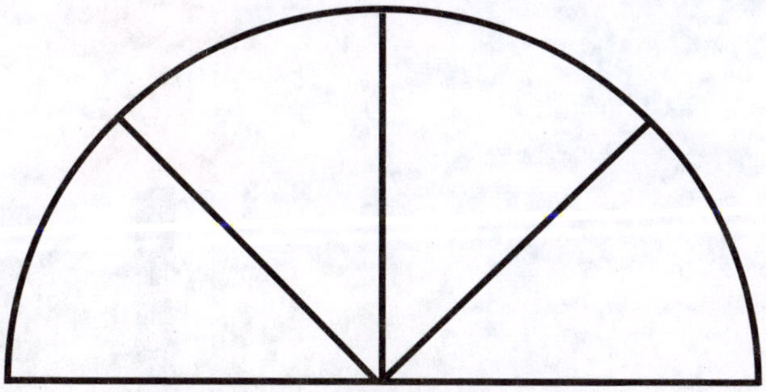

c.

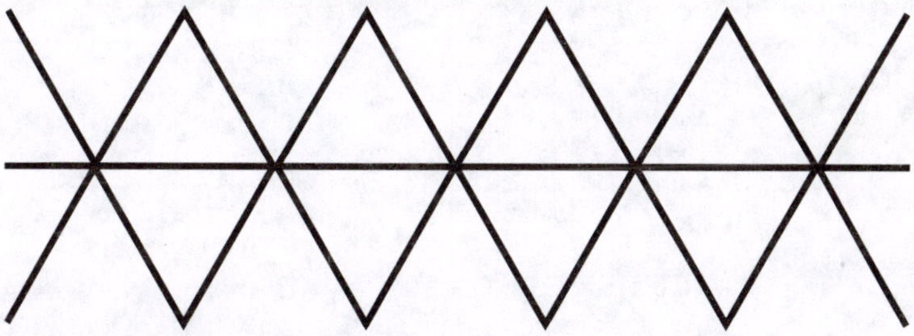

d.

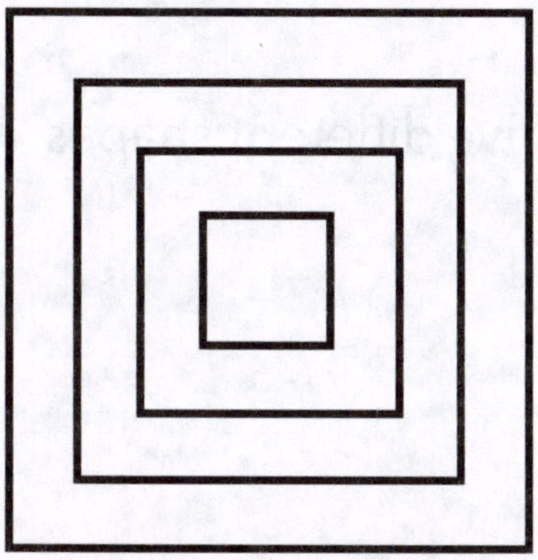

e.

5. Count and write the number of each shape.

Projects

1. Create a scenery in MS Paint using at least five different shapes.
2. Draw three patterns using the MS Paint.

Introduction to Tux Typing

Tux Typing is a typing program. It makes us familiar with the keys present on the keyboard. It is used to learn typing on a keyboard.

STARTING TUX TYPING

To start Tux Typing, Click on the Start button then type 'Tux Typing' in the search bar. Alternatively, you can also double-click on the 'Tux Typing' shortcut on the desktop.

Tux Typing Window

The main menu of the Tux Typing window shows many options. These are:

1. **Fish Cascade**: Opens the Fish Cascade game.
2. **Comet Zap**: Opens the Comet Zap game.
3. **Lessons**: Shows typing lessons that users can use to learn typing.
4. **Options**: Allows users to change the language.
5. **Quit**: Closes the program.

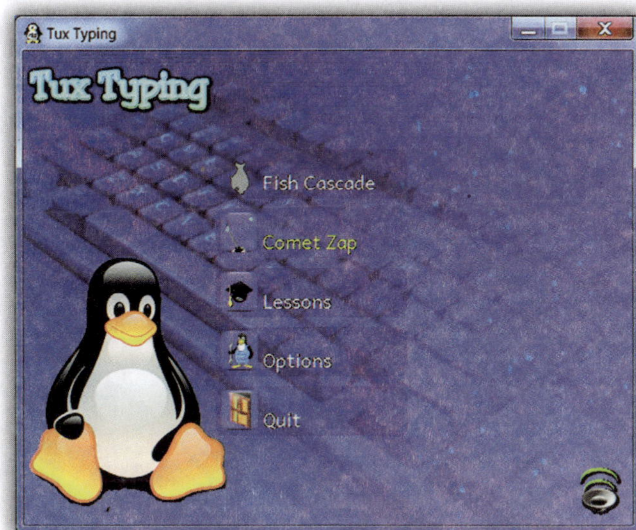

Fig. 1 *Tux Typing window*

Knowledge Bytes

When we type on the keyboard, every finger has a special role. Practice typing by placing the fingers on the keys as shown in this picture.

GAMES IN TUX TYPING

Tux Typing has two games Fish Cascade and Comet Zap. Let us see how these games are played.

Fish Cascade

In this game, users need to press the alphabet written on the falling fish so that the penguin can eat them. If users fail to type the correct alphabet, the penguin loses one life. The game ends when the penguin loses all his lives.

I am smart!

If a user presses the wrong key, the penguin loses it's lives, thus the game is over.

To start the Fish Cascade game, follow these steps:

1. Click on the **Fish Cascade** option (Fig. 2).

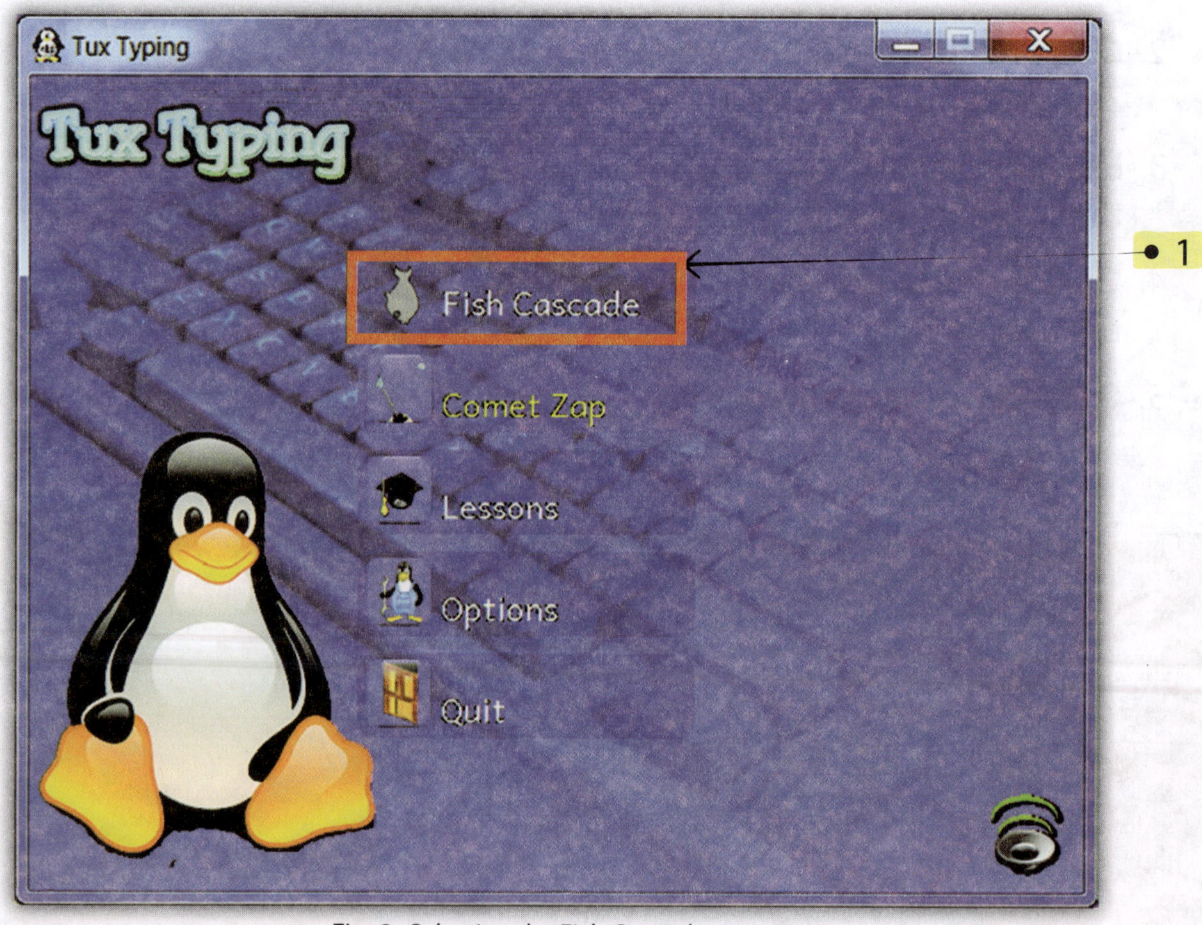

Fig. 2 *Selecting the Fish Cascade option*

2. Choose the level of the game, say **Easy** (Fig. 3).

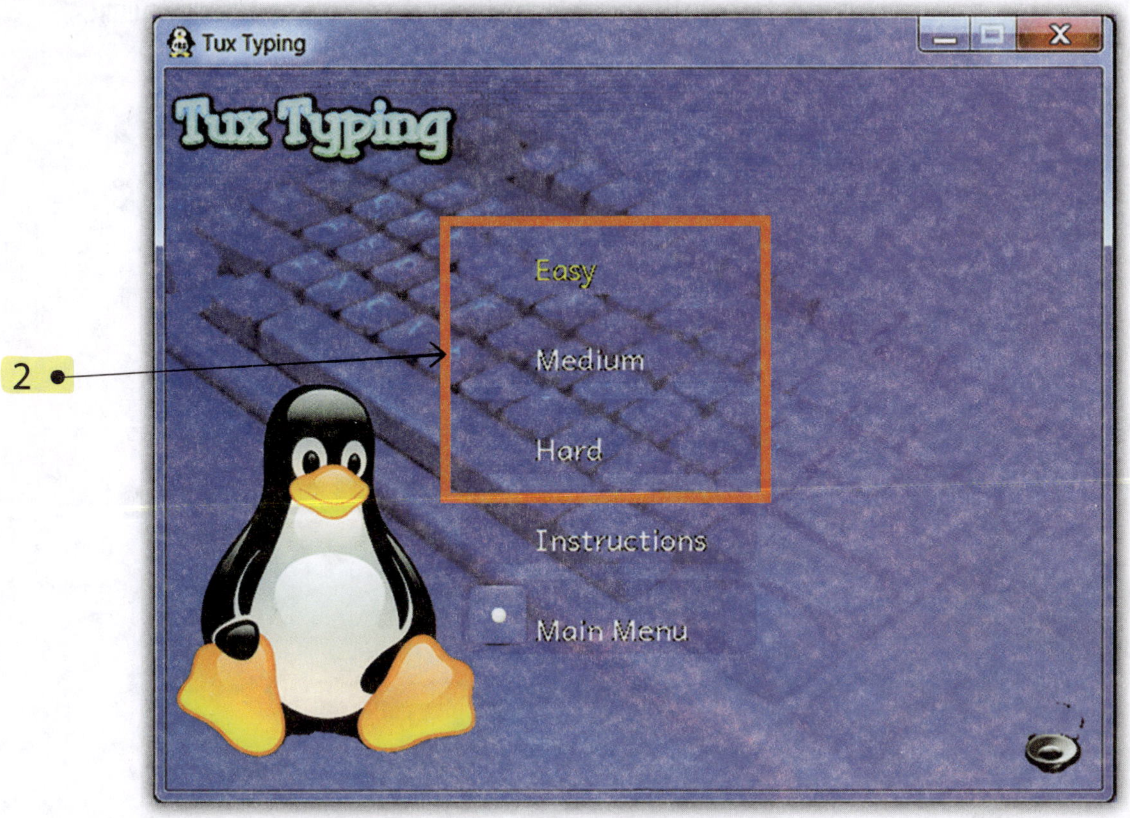

Fig. 3 *Selecting a level*

3. Choose the theme, say **Alphabet** (Fig. 4).

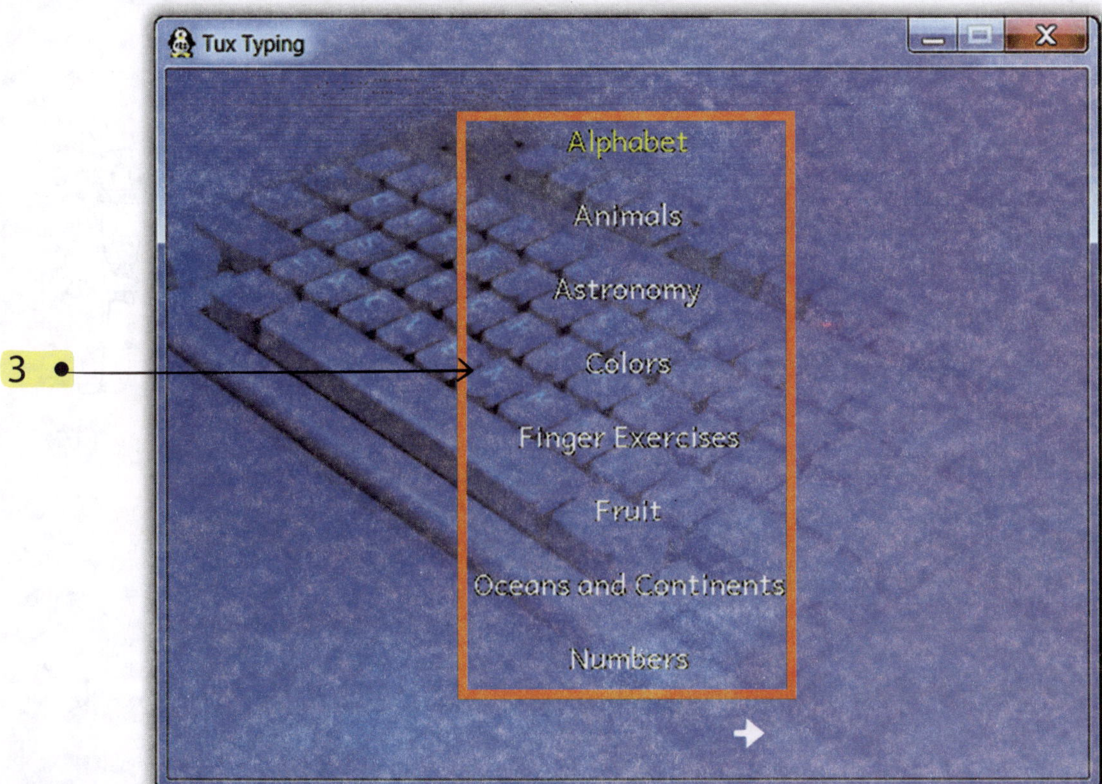

Fig. 4 *Selecting a theme*

4. Type the letter(s) written on the falling fish before it reaches the ground (Fig. 5).

4 •

Fig. 5 *Playing Fish Cascade*

Comet Zap

In Comet Zap, the penguin needs to shoot the comets that are coming to hit the city. Users need to press the correct alphabets or words written on the comets so that the penguin can shoot the comets, save his city and score points. The game ends when the comets destroy the city.

To start the Comet Zap game, follow these steps

1. Click on the **Comet Zap** option (Fig. 6).

I am smart!

- Press Esc key from the keyboard to pause the game.
- Pressing the Esc key twice takes us back to the Main Menu.

Fig. 6 *Selecting the* Comet Zap *option*

Fig. 7 *Selecting the type of background and comet*

2. Choose the type of background and comet, say **Pilot** (Fig. 7).

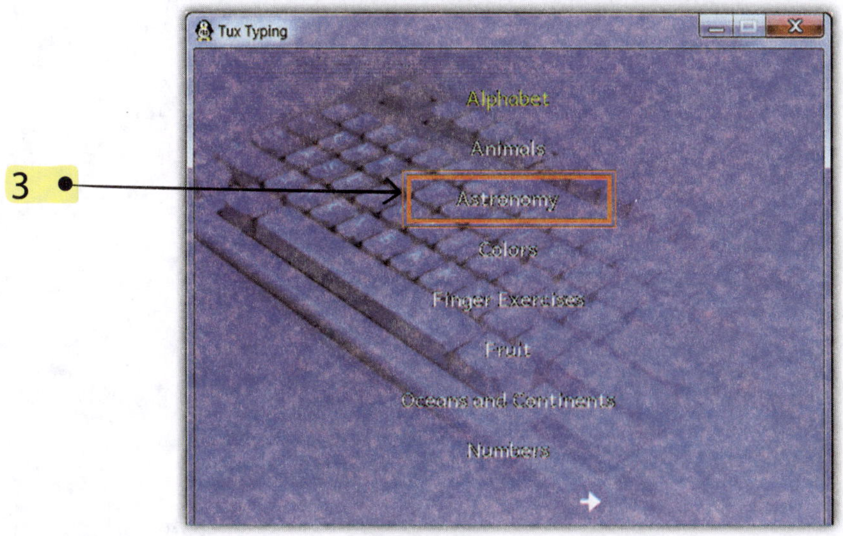

Fig. 8 *Choosing a theme*

3. Choose the theme, say **Astronomy** (Fig. 8).

4. Type the alphabet(s) written on the falling comets before it destroys the city (Fig. 9).

Fig. 9 *Playing the game*

Lessons

Tux Typing has 43 lessons. These lessons cover almost all the characters on the keyboard. These lessons help in understanding the various keys on the keyboard. To start the **Lessons**, follow these steps (Fig. 10):

1. Click on the **Lessons** option.
2. Choose the lesson, say **basic_ lesson_01.xml**. A new screen appears.
3. Press the **Spacebar** key to start the lesson. A new screen appears.
4. Press the ***p*** key to start practice.
5. Press the marked character with the finger suggested by red dot.

Fig. 10 *Selecting the Lessons option*

2. Choose the lesson, say **basic_ lesson_01.xml**. A new screen appears (Fig. 11).

Fig. 11 *Choosing a lesson*

3. Press the **Spacebar** key to start the lesson. A new screen appears (Fig. 12).

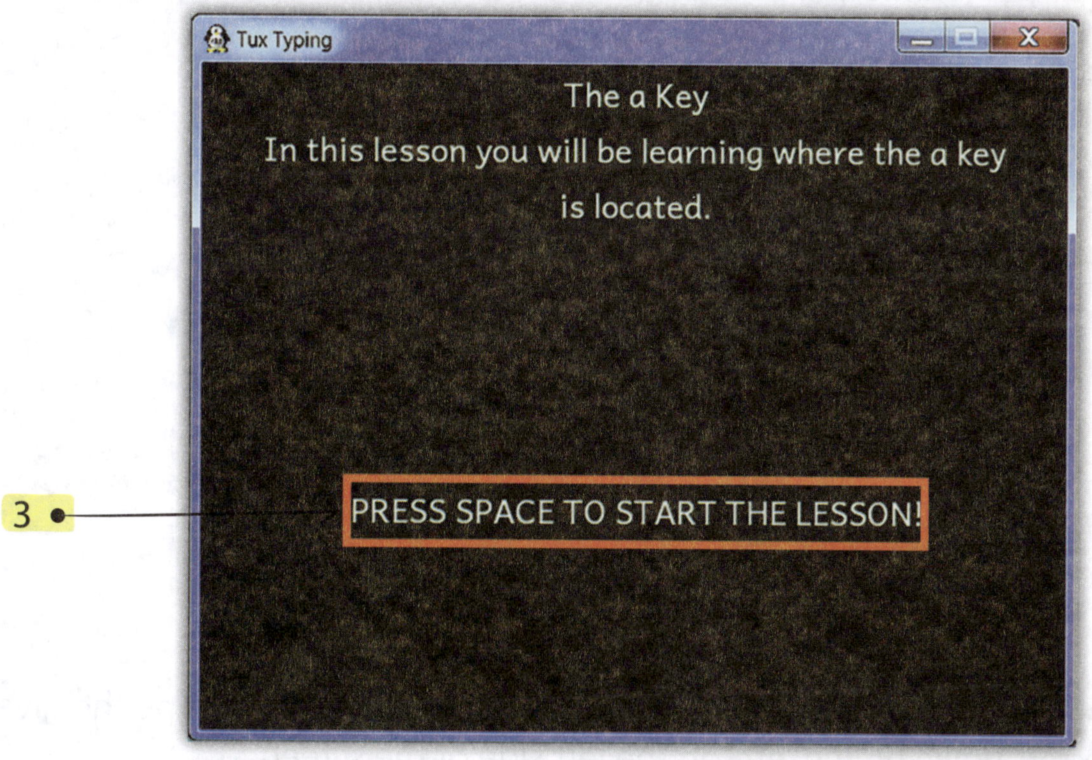

Fig. 12 *Pressing a key*

4. Press the ***p*** key to start the practice (Fig. 13).

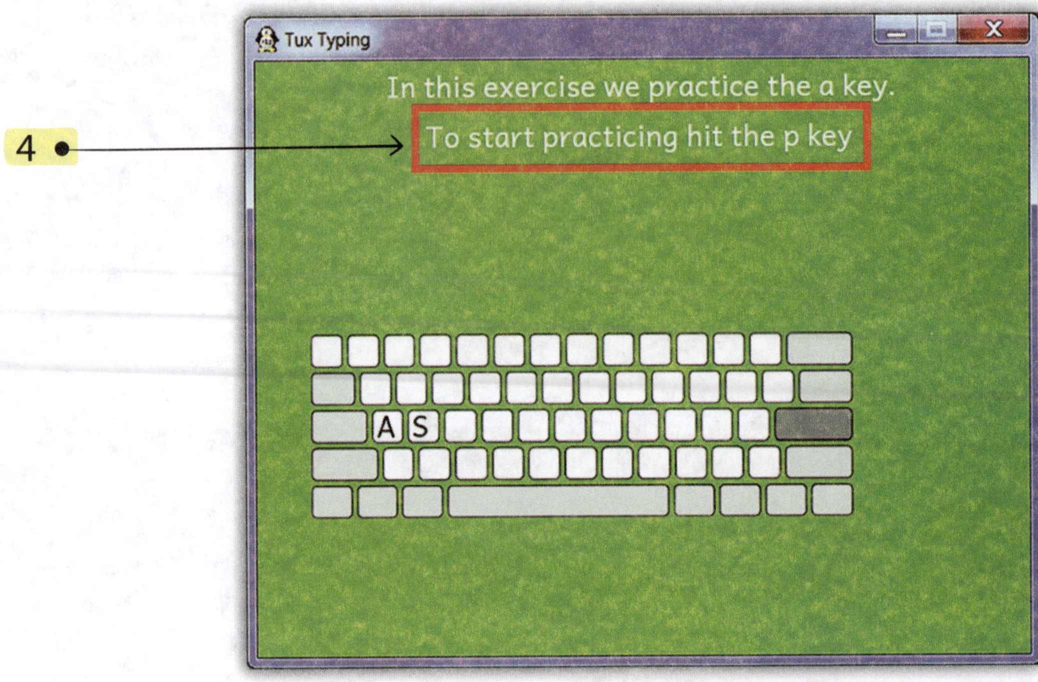

Fig. 13 *Starting the practice*

5. Press the marked character with the finger suggested by red dot (Fig. 14).

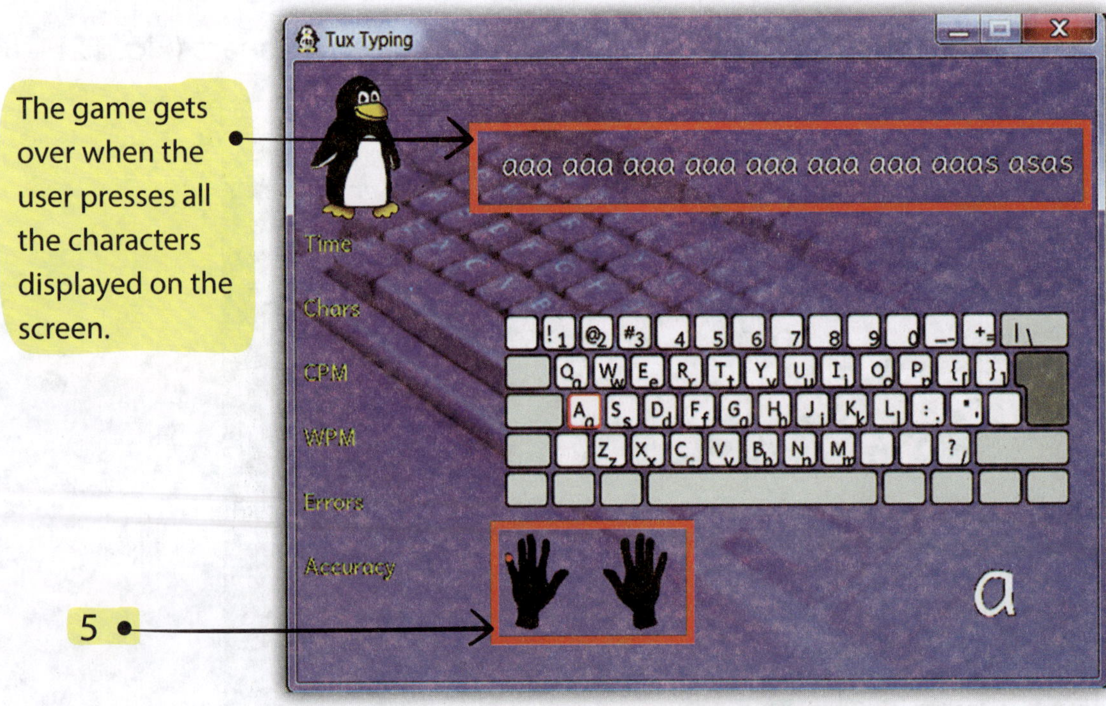

Fig. 14 *Lessons in Tux Typing*

Tux Typing also displays the performance in terms of time taken to type the given characters, errors while typing, etc. on the left side of the screen.

Fun Time

Help Rajeev to play the Comet Zap game by numbering the given steps in the correct order.

Choose the theme, say Astronomy. [ ]

Click on the Comet Zap option. [ ]

Type the alphabet(s) written on the falling comets. [ ]

Choose the type of background and comet, say Pilot. [ ]

Lab Activity

1. Play Fish Cascade and Comet Zap with your partner in the computer lab.
2. Start with the Easy level, and then move to the Medium and Hard levels. Also, keep watching the scores.

Group Discussion

Divide the class into two groups and discuss the following.

1. How is Tux Typing is an interesting program?
2. Does it really improve typing?

Click on https://tux-typing.en.uptodown.com/windows to download Tux Typing.

Using a Computer Properly

1. Sit comfortably with back straight. Do not lean forward or slouch.		

✓	✗	✗

2. Maintain proper distance from the monitor. Sitting too close may affect your eyesight. The room you are in should be well lit.		

✗	✗	✓

3. Ensure that the keyboard and the mouse are at the correct height. The monitor should be level with your eyes.		

✗	✗	✓

4. If your feet do not reach the floor, place a footstool under your feet.

✗	✓	✓

5. While listening to sounds coming from the computer, use headphones. This will not disturb others.

✗	✓

6. Take a 5-minute break after very 20-30 minutes. Lean back in your chair with your eyes closed for 20 seconds. Get up from your chair and walk for a few minutes.

✓	✓

About the Authors

Sneha Krishnan and **Manasi Kashikar**, techies at heart, bond over their love of coding. They are co-founders of the company *MindChamp* where they teach coding to school students using fun, activity-based learning. They both love to teach students and that reflects in their work. Together with a team of educators, they have taught thousands of students to create computer games and websites. They want to make coding accessible to young students as well, so they are better equipped for the future.